GOD & MAMMON

Asking for Money in the New Testament

Jouette M. Bassler

ABINGDON PRESS
Nashville

GOD AND MAMMON: ASKING FOR MONEY IN THE NEW TESTAMENT

Library of Congress Cataloging-in-Publication Data

Bassler, Jouette M.
    God and mammon : asking for money in the New Testament / Jouette M. Bassler.
        p.   cm.
    Includes bibliographical references and index.
    ISBN 0-687-14962-2 (pbk. : alk. paper)
    1. Church fund raising—Biblical teaching. 2. Money—Biblical teaching.
3. Bible. N.T.—Criticism, interpretation, etc.
I. Title.
BS2545.C554B37   1991
253.8—dc20   90-48508
                                                                         CIP

MANUFACTURED IN THE UNITED STATES OF AMERICA

In memory of my grandmother,
Minnie Martin Flack,
who wove the Hundredth Psalm
into the fabric of her life.

CONTENTS

T his book was written for people who would like to reflect more deeply on the theological and ethical aspects of fund-raising in the church but might not know where to begin. There are many places that one might begin, but I suggest that one of the most fruitful is the New Testament. I have selected some New Testament texts on asking for money (there are very few of them) and have tried to present them so that the theological and ethical issues they raise are clear. To uncover these issues I have used the tools and insights of New Testament scholarship, but I have not presupposed that readers will have had formal training in this field. The suggestions for further reading presented at the end of each chapter list the scholars whose work has been most influential on the analyses presented here as well as scholars whose conclusions differ from my own. Readers whose interest is piqued by this book will find resources here for further study.

Some readers may be disappointed because I do not give firm pronouncements or even clear advice about the application of these texts to the situation of today's churches (though doubtless there are frequent clues to where my preferences lie). It was never my intention to do this. Instead I hope to stimulate readers to do their own theological reflecting on the activity of asking for money by showing the evidence and fruits of this activity within the New Testament.

In an attempt to facilitate this reflecting, I have provided some discussion questions for each chapter. There is always the danger that these questions reflect my own interests and concerns more than those of readers, so they should not be taken as either definitive or exhaustive. The questions are simply intended to encourage thinking about fund-raising issues of our own churches in the light of these New Testament texts. I hope that disagreement with my reading of the texts—and there is bound to be some disagreement—will not deflect attention from the goal we all share: how the church can engage in the necessary task of asking for money in a way that is faithful to its mission and call.

I would like to express my gratitude to the members of the Tuesday night Bible study group of Ridgeview Presbyterian Church in Dallas, Texas, and especially to Jann Treadwell, who invited me to address this group. It was to them that I first presented my ideas on this topic, and their enthusiasm as well as their honest criticisms have been invaluable to me as I worked to bring the project to completion. I was provided generous financial assistance for this task by a Faculty Development Grant from the Lilly Endowment. Further encouragement and stimulation was provided by the Commission on Stewardship of the Ecumenical Center for Stewardship Studies, which provided me with a fellowship to attend its 1988 Colloquy for Theological Educators. I am grateful both to the Commission and to its director, Ronald E. Vallet, for this encouragement. A colleague, C. Clifton Black, read the manuscript and provided many helpful suggestions. My deepest thanks, however, go to my husband John, who read countless drafts with consummate patience. Whatever the book possesses in the way of clarity and grace is due to his keen eye and careful appraisal. By rights the book should be dedicated to him, but *this* one is for my grandmother. In countless ways it is her book, and I think she might even have enjoyed reading it.

You cannot serve God and mammon.
—*Matthew 6:24* (RSV)

You never ever ever get away from the pressure
that you have to raise funds for the next
week, the next month, the next year.
—*Jim Bakker*

The subject matter of this book is rooted deep in my past. It goes back, I think, to my grandmother. Completely without financial resources of her own, she lived with my family as I was growing up. Late in her life when she could no longer get around very well, television personalities became her particular friends. The world of the soap operas was at least as real for her as the world of the block we lived on, and she could never resist a television evangelist. She would send a ten-dollar bill to anyone who asked for money "in the name of Jesus." My mother, knowing my grandmother's financial straits, would always retrieve the letter from the mailbox and return the ten-dollar bill to my grandmother's purse, where it was ready to send to the next evangelist who asked.

In those days television preachers were an occasional phenomenon. Today one can hardly escape them. At almost any time of the day or night one can find on some channel the familiar figure, the familiar voice, and the familiar plea to send money "in the name of Jesus." We do not really need the evidence of the Bakkers and the Swaggarts to realize that something is fundamentally askew here. Raising money has become an end, not a means, an end that seems to justify *any* means.

Though highlighted by some television ministries, this is an issue that affects all churches. All churches need money to perform their ministries, yet asking for money in the name of Jesus raises—or should raise—some serious questions. What constraints do those words, "in the name of Jesus," place on our fund-raising activities? May churches use the tactics of the secular world to bring the necessary funds into their coffers? Or does the church's special call and commission bring a different dimension to the task of acquiring unholy mammon? It is with these questions in mind that I propose to turn back to the early Christian documents and see what they have to say about how the church is to carry out its necessary task of asking for money.

We should not be so naive as to think that we will find there easy answers to the difficult question of what ethical or theological constraints should be placed on the activity of asking for money. In the first place, these documents reflect a world very different from our own. Our social, economic, and cultural experiences are quite different from those of people who lived in the first-century Mediterranean world, yet it is to these people that the New Testament documents were initially directed. Thus we cannot take over the message of these texts without an act of cultural translation. In the second place, the various New Testament documents present different answers to our questions. Each document was written for a different community, with different needs and different questions and even different understandings of the practice of asking for money. In short, the New Testament speaks with many voices, all of them in some way different from our own.

The documents also reveal, however, that in many ways the situation of the church in the first century was remarkably like the situation today. Missionary and benevolence programs required financing, congregations had bills to pay, ministerial staffs needed recompense. Thus almost from the beginning of the Christian movement there was a tension between an awareness of the corrupting power of money and the need to generate it. And since the religious charlatan was present almost from the start, there was also a need for Christians to distinguish themselves and their appeals for money from those whose appeals were less high-minded. It cannot hurt, then, to engage in active dialogue with the foundation documents of our faith about the practice of asking for money.

Because of this focus on money, our study falls within the general category of stewardship. There are many books, of course, on this topic, whether conceived broadly as a stewardship of life or more narrowly as a stewardship of possessions and money, and most of these devote at least one chapter to the biblical bases of the concept. Because this present study seems to cover much the same ground, most of it already thoroughly tilled, I should set out what distinguishes this work from its predecessors. First, my aim is rather different. I do not intend to look at New Testament texts that are relevant to stewardship as a way of life. For that topic, the entire canon would need to be considered! Nor do I intend to explore texts relevant to the more narrowly construed issue of stewardship as responsible giving. Even this would involve a large number of texts covering topics ranging from the beneficence of God to the meaning of faith. Instead I will address the relatively few New Testament texts that speak directly to the question of *asking* for money. To be sure, there will be some overlap here, for texts that feature requests for money often support the request by presenting various motives for giving. But it is the activity of asking *per se* that concerns us here. We will look at texts that either contain an explicit request for money (or its equivalent) or describe an activity that has implicit in it such a request.

The second point at which this study differs from most stewardship studies is in its methodology. So often when biblical texts are cited to illustrate an aspect of stewardship, no consideration is given to the circumstances in which these texts originally functioned. They float, as it were, in a cultural and social vacuum, and we get no sense of the factors that led to a specific request or its social consequences. Yet it is precisely this information, I believe, that allows the texts to take on life and meaning. It is when we hear these texts speaking most clearly in their original settings that they begin to speak most effectively to us today. To be sure, what we may discover is that some of these texts are so closely tied to these settings that they cannot be translated into a word for our time. Learning this is, I think, preferable to doing violence to their intent by forcibly applying them to an irreconcilably different situation. Thus I propose that we approach the question of what the New Testament texts on asking for money have to say to us today through the back door of listening to what they said in their original historical and social and cultural settings. The route may seem indirect and the way difficult, but until we can hear these texts against their original backdrops, our appreciation of them will be superficial and our appropriation of them *could* be misguided.

This means that we will be engaging in a difficult dialogue with these texts. The original setting of a saying is not always immediately obvious. Sometimes it needs to be painstakingly pieced together through historical reconstruction and sociological analysis. And we need to approach the task with minds as open as possible. There may emerge from this dialogue some suggestions that are alien or even offensive to us today. It will not help our understanding to sugar-coat such texts with piety. Instead we need to listen to them all the more intently, and if the dialogue causes us to look more closely at our own practices and to think more seriously and more theologically about their implications, the dialogue will have been worthwhile. So let us listen to some New Testament texts, realizing that we may or may not find answers suitable to our situation, but we should emerge from the dialogue more sensitive to the problem.

We will open our study of the fund-raising practices of the early Christians with a survey of the world in which they lived and traveled and made their requests for money. This is not primarily the Jewish world of Palestine, for the energy of the Christian movement and the heart of the Christian mission soon shifted to the Gentile world of the Roman Empire. This was a complex world, nearly as complex as our own, and we cannot hope to cover all facets of it. Instead we will focus on those social interactions where money was requested or delivered.

We are not concerned, of course, with the exchanges of money for goods or services that are always a part of daily life, but with outright requests for gifts of money, whether for large sums or small. Who made these requests? On what grounds were they made? Were there any ethical or philosophical or theological restraints to the practice in the non-Christian world? Christianity did not grow in a vacuum. Other people in the environment of early Christianity engaged in the practice of asking for money, and how they did it and what they had to say about it may shed light on the New Testament texts that address this question. They must become part of our dialogue.

Who, then, was asking for money? We can be sure that requests for money occurred up and down the entire social scale of the ancient world, on street corners, in modest homes, and in palatial estates. Unfortunately, few of the people making these requests thought it necessary or worthwhile to record their thoughts on the activity. It was as necessary, in some ways, as breathing, and as uninteresting to reflect on. Yet some of them did, and we can sample their reflections from both ends of the social scale.

At one end of the social spectrum were the beggars, and the writings of this period suggest that they were a familiar and annoying sight. But the indigent do not write. They were, for the most part, nameless and voiceless and did not leave behind any reflections on their actions. They begged out of need, then ate and begged again. For most, that is all we know. One group of mendicants, however, were beggars on principle, not out of need. They were also educated and literate, followers, they said, of Socrates. They had their critics, of course, who left behind some rather caustic comments about their motives. But these philosophical beggars, known as Cynics, penned their own documents, providing philosophical and theological justification for the life-style they had embraced.

At the other end of the social spectrum from these beggars were the wealthy. These were often benefactors on a large scale, giving money not to individuals but to cities, societies, or guilds. While they too left few writings reflecting on their actions, the recipients of their largess often recorded their gratitude on monuments of stone. Indeed, the praise inscribed there is so lavish that it often amounts to a thinly veiled request for more money. Thus these formal but effusive expressions of gratitude can provide us with information about the dynamics of giving and receiving that operated at the upper end of the social scale in the world of the early Christian church. After this introduction we will turn to the documents of the early church.

We will begin this part of the study by considering what light the gospels throw on the practice of asking for money. Only in Jesus' mission instructions to the twelve apostles is there relevant information, and we need to assess it very carefully. The instructions reflect the ethos of a distinctive group of Jesus' followers, and only by pushing behind the gospels can we adequately explore the implications of the instructions. Furthermore, there is evidence in the gospels that the basic attitude was modified in the light of changing circumstances. We need to be attentive to these developments.

Paul's letters provide the richest sources of information on asking for money. The apostle distinguished between two modes of asking—asking for money for personal support and asking for contributions for a collection for the poor in Jerusalem. Various pressures that were placed on Paul forced him to subject both modes of asking to careful scrutiny, and in his letters we can listen to him both defend his position on asking for money and engage in actual requests. In both cases he proves to be sensitive to the theological and ethical issues involved. Finally, the book of Acts contains no explicit references to asking for money, but the community of goods that Acts ascribes to the early church imposes an expectation of giving that is tantamount to a request. We can best uncover the implications of this request through a literary analysis of the opening chapters in Acts that is sensitive to the social dynamics suggested by the narrative.

The aim of this study is not to suggest a normative approach to fund-raising. The first-century world of the Mediterranean would be a strange place indeed to seek that! Rather, the aim is to stimulate theological reflection on the activity by exploring how some early Christian writers in a world at once like and unlike our own tried to reconcile the need to ask for money with the fundamental tenets of their faith.

FOR FURTHER READING

There are a number of works on the broader issue of stewardship, and most of these devote some attention to New Testament texts. None focuses on *asking*, and few engage the biblical texts with exegetical rigor, but all offer some helpful insights. Otto A. Piper, for example, a New Testament scholar, wrote *The Christian Meaning of Money* (Englewood Cliffs, N.J.: Prentice-Hall, 1965) to explore what modern financial activities look like in the light of the Bible. His surprisingly brief survey of the biblical view does not, however, suggest the diversity of viewpoints found in the Bible. Holmes Rolston's book *Stewardship in the New Testament Church* (Richmond: John Knox Press, 1946) has gone through two editions and numerous reprintings. The strength of this book, which focuses on the New Testament world, lies not so much in its analysis of the texts as in its

15

sensitivity to questions and concerns that arise in the modern church.

The essays collected in a book edited by T. K. Thompson, *Stewardship in Contemporary Theology* (New York: Association Press, 1960), include entries on the Old Testament, the teachings of Jesus, and the philosophy of Paul, but they are brief and rather superficial. A second volume edited by Thompson, *Stewardship in Contemporary Life* (New York: Association Press, 1965), contains a pair of essays by James M. Gustafson that raise some provocative questions about the ethics of various fund-raising and evangelization activities. Gustafson does not, however, place the ethical questions that he raises within a biblical perspective. Theophilus M. Taylor's essay in the same volume, on the other hand, surveys, but does not analyze, the various motives for giving found in the New Testament.

Helge Brattgård's study entitled *God's Stewards,* translated by G. J. Lund (Minneapolis, Minn.: Augsburg, 1963), provides careful, contextual analyses of biblical texts and sensitive theological observations. It was written for the Lutheran World Federation and explores the Lutheran creeds in some depth, but all can benefit from its insights. Richard B. Cunningham's book *Creative Stewardship* (Nashville: Abingdon, 1979) is much more practically oriented, and though salted with references to biblical texts, it does not attempt a careful analysis of any of them.

CHAPTER 1

PERSPECTIVES FROM THE ANCIENT WORLD: BEGGARS AND BENEFACTORS

I have no right to deny the stranger. . . . All vagabonds
and strangers are under Zeus.
—Homer, The Odyssey, *xiv*, 56-57

We begin our survey of requests for money in the ancient world with Homer's epic poem. Politically the world of the early Christians was Roman, but culturally it was still Greek, and the figure of Odysseus was important in that world. The pronouncement quoted above from that epic would thus seem to suggest a powerful cultural tolerance for the life-style of the beggar, the "stranger" who lived by asking for money. But Odysseus was hardly a typical beggar. He was a vagabond of exceptional circumstances and heroic dimensions, who adopted the garb of a beggar only in direst need as he struggled to make his way home to Ithaca to reclaim his wife and throne. Moreover, the pronouncement does not prove to be a cultural force even in the world of the poem, for those who caught no glimmer of Odysseus' regal nature responded to his begging in the more expected vein of hostility and fear. Thus *The Odyssey* presents a paradox: a pronouncement of divine protection for *all* vagabonds and strangers, but this is applied only to one who is a vagabond *extraordinaire*. The epic provides no concrete model for dealing with those who begged because of chronic destitution rather than heroic need. Did Homer's umbrella of divine protection influence attitudes in the real world of unheroic poverty and need? Were real vagabonds, with their life-style of begging, viewed as being somehow "under Zeus"? We need to understand the attitudes toward begging in this period in order to understand the comments of those who lived by asking for money.

ATTITUDES TOWARD BEGGING IN THE GRECO-ROMAN WORLD

The world of the Mediterranean basin in the centuries surrounding the birth of Christianity was more populous and infinitely more complex than the world of Homer's fable. There were real urban centers complete with blighting poverty. Travel was commonplace and not only beggars, *real* beggars, but also priests from various religious cults, fortune tellers, hucksters, and swindlers of all sorts took to the roads, asking for money in the name of charity, piety, or gullibility. In this world Homer's words about the hospitality due to the wandering beggar hardly seemed relevant or reasonable.

In the fourth century B.C. Aristotle still extolled generosity as the appropriate attitude in dealing with money and other material goods, but it was a cautious sort of generosity that he envisioned. In Book 4 of his *Nicomachean Ethics,* Aristotle describes the generous or "liberal" person as one who navigates the ideal mean between the opposing extremes of extravagance and miserliness. Unlike the extravagant, who are careless with money and possessions, and unlike the miserly, who care too much for them, generous persons give liberally yet in proportion to their possessions. They give gladly for the sheer goodness or nobility of giving and derive pleasure from the deed. But they do *not* give to just anyone who asks! They give only "to the right people, and the right amount, and at the right time." Aristotle also noted that the generous person would *take* money only from proper sources as well, but he was much more interested in the ethics of giving than those of receiving. His firm and influential conclusion was that one gives to the right people, to people of good character, and not to the wrong ones, for some people simply deserve to be poor (4.1).

We can hear echoes of this sentiment in subsequent centuries. Cicero, for example, a Roman orator and statesman who lived from 106 to 43 B.C., advised a moderate approach to giving that reflects Aristotle's ideal mean: "One's purse should not be closed so tightly that a generous impulse cannot open it, nor yet so loosely held as to be open to everybody" (*On Duties* 2.15.55). A century later Seneca, a wealthy Roman philosopher and moralist, wrote an essay entitled "On the Happy Life" in which he vigorously—and somewhat self-servingly—defended the ownership of wealth and recommended utmost deliberation and caution when giving to others. The wealthy person, he said, "will give of [his wealth] either to good men or to those whom he is able to make good men; choosing the most worthy after the utmost deliberation" (*Moral Essay* 7.23.5).

Classical scholar A. R. Hands has noted that in the parlance of the time, worth and goodness were qualities of the educated upper classes. Upper-class Greeks, he says, could not conceive of goodness as compatible with real poverty. The Roman attitude seems similar. Cicero, at least, regularly equated the indigent with the wicked, the base, the squalid, the corrupt, and the incorrigible. Thus when Aristotle and Seneca and Cicero recommended giving to the deserving, the worthy, and the good, they were urging their readers to give *only to people like themselves,* people of the educated elite who, through some reversal of fortune, had descended from prosperity to (relative) poverty. To *these* people the generous person's hand was always extended, for who could know when their positions might be reversed? As for the chronically poor and the indigent beggars, they were viewed as deserving their poverty, not financial aid.

This profoundly negative judgment on poverty and especially on the life of the beggar is what made the mendicant philosophers known as Cynics so distinctive and outrageous in their time. They voluntarily adopted the life-style of the despised beggar and defended it in the face of the inevitable criticisms that arose. Who were these philosophers and what did they say about the practice of asking for alms?

The Mendicant Philosophers

When we use the word "cynic" today, we usually have in mind a chronic faultfinder who will acknowledge no decent motive to any human action. This usage captures the critical spirit of the ancient Cynics, but only on the most superficial level. Cynics were, after all, philosophers, though not in the speculative mode of Plato or Aristotle. They were interested in how people lived, in ethics, and what they taught was more a way of life than a philosophical system. Their origins are somewhat cloudy, but it was clearly Diogenes in the fourth century B.C. who established the way of life that all subsequent Cynics more or less followed. (I say "more or less" because, as we will see, there was considerable diversity among Cynics as well as quite a number of charlatans.) This life-style was based on the conviction that the goal of human life was a state of inner peace or happiness, where one is free from internal passions or external changes in fortune. The way to this state was through self-sufficiency, and the way to self-sufficiency was through a simple and natural style of life. "It is the privilege of the gods," Diogenes is quoted as saying, "to need nothing, and of god-like men to want but little" (Diogenes Laertius, *Lives of Eminent Philosophers* 6.104). Some Cynics, however, were more god-like than others. Diogenes, for example, pursued the life-style of the gods with ascetic rigor, reducing his physical needs to an alarming minimum— water, a simple diet of grains or lentils, a single cloak. Others, like his pupil Crates, were milder in their interpretation of the natural life-style, and some even drifted toward hedonism. Whether mild or rigorous, Cynics combined their simple life with a blazing indictment of the luxury, greed, and hypocrisy of their society. This attack they carried out with such boldness, insolence, and occasional shamelessness that they earned the name "Dogs" ("Cynics"), a scurrilous label that they wore as a badge of honor.

Most Cynics lived by begging for their modest needs. In fact, their trademark became the begging-bag, which together with a staff for protection and a single cloak (folded once in summer, twice in winter) made up their entire possessions. They were a distinctive feature of Greek society in the third century B.C., uncompromising in their morals, brazen in their language, and occasionally offensive in their life-style. As a countercultural movement they eventually faded from view, but their message of simple frugality was absorbed by the more moderate and more acceptable Stoic philosophy.

In the first century of the Christian era, Cynic beggars appeared again in the cities and on the roads of the Roman Empire. This time, however, these eccentric but serious critics of luxury and ostentation were joined by impostors who used the Cynic begging-bag as a means for satisfying their greed. So numerous were these impostors that the Cynics acquired a reputation not only for brazen criticism but also for greed and hypocrisy, the very attitudes the true Cynic attacked. This confusion and corruption of the movement generated severe criticism by first and second-century moralists, who identified begging with false philosophers.

Criticism of the Cynics

Criticism of the Cynics came from many directions, but some of the most caustic comments came from the pen of Lucian, a second-century satirist who combined wit and outrage in his virulent attacks. In a comic dialogue entitled "The Runaways" he presented Philosophy, daughter of Zeus, complaining to her father. Some miscreants, she says, "an abominable class of men . . . slaves and hirelings," were besmirching her name and reputation among the people.

21

With no philosophical training or education and motivated solely by greed, this "army of the dog" had donned the short cloak and taken up the staff and begging-bag, and were shouting, braying, and howling in the marketplace, slandering everyone in sight. She goes on to describe their behavior:

> Bread, too, is no longer scanty or, as before, limited to bannocks of barley; and what goes with it is not salt fish or thyme but meat of all sorts and wine of the sweetest, and money from whomsoever they will; for they collect tribute, going from house to house, or, as they themselves express it, they "shear the sheep"; and they expect many to give, either out of respect for their cloth or for fear of their abusive language. ("Runaways" 14)

These men are pure frauds, Philosophy concludes, more jackass than dog. Lucian addressed the same theme in another essay entitled "The Fisherman." Here Philosophy looks in a Cynic's begging-bag expecting to find a book or a simple loaf of bread. Instead she finds gold and perfume, a razor, a mirror, and a set of dice. "Did you think," she asks contemptuously, "that with the aid of these you could . . . instruct the rest of the world?" ("Fisherman" 45).

Others also complained of the greed and degeneracy of the Cynic movement. Dio Chrysostom, for example, a Greek rhetorician of the first century A.D., for a while actually lived the life of the Cynic philosopher. Yet in an oration to the people of Alexandria he assailed the impostors who post "themselves at street-corners, in alley-ways, and at temple gates, pass round the hat and play upon the credulity of lads and sailors and crowds of that sort . . . [and] accustom thoughtless people to deride philosophers in general" (*Discourse* 32.9). Epictetus, a Stoic philosopher of the same era, was also much taken by the Cynic life of simplicity. He praises the ideal Cynic in his essay "On the Calling of a Cynic," but he also includes words of scorn for those who thought that "what makes a Cynic is a contemptible wallet [begging-bag], a staff, and big jaws; to devour everything you give him, or to stow it away, or to revile tactlessly the people he meets, or to show off his fine shoulder" (*Discourses* 3.22.50). The Roman philosopher Seneca held one Cynic named Demetrius in highest esteem. In general, however, he found it outrageous that people who claimed to despise money should go about asking for it (*On Benefits* 2.17.2). All of these voices are simply repeating the opinion Epicurus had expressed some centuries earlier: The true sage will not beg or live as a Cynic (Diogenes Laertius, *Lives of Eminent Philosophers* 10.119). In general, then, the simple life-style of the Cynics was admired. It was their practice of asking for money that brought the movement into disrepute.

The Cynic Response: The Ethics of Begging

True Cynics, then, had to distinguish and dissociate themselves from the charlatans and hucksters who imitated their life-style. This meant that either they had to give up their practice of begging or, if they retained it, they had to defend the practice in the face of this persistent criticism. We can see their attempt to deal with these problems in some letters attributed to Diogenes, Crates, and other well-known Cynics. These letters are hard to date with any precision. They claim as their authors the founding figures of the Cynic movement who lived in the fourth and third centuries B.C., but scholars have demonstrated that they were actually written much later during the resurgence of Cynicism in the first and second centuries A.D. The appeal to Diogenes and other early Cynics was thus an attempt to gain credibility for the letters, which were written to counter the later criticism of the Cynic movement. (I will use quotation marks when referring to the "authors" of these letters to remind us of this literary hoax.) Better than any other documents we have, these letters reveal how the Cynics (at least those in the first century A.D.) justified on philosophical and ethical grounds their practice of asking for alms.

One argument with a characteristically brazen twist appears repeatedly in defense of Cynic begging. By the time of Aristotle, it had been established as a maxim that friends held all things in common. The Cynics used this maxim to devise a syllogism to justify their begging. With slight variations, it goes like this. All things belong to God; friends have things in common; only the Cynic sage or philosopher is a friend of God; therefore when the Cynic sage begs, he is not asking for something that belongs to others but is demanding back what already belongs to him ("Crates" Epp. 26, 27; "Diogenes" Ep. 10). (Though nothing prevented women from joining the Cynics, only one, Hypparchia, is known actually to have done so. The use of the masculine pronoun, then, reflects the overwhelming masculinity of the movement.) The argument is clever, if not logically convincing, but what is it actually saying? Critics of the practice, you recall, had described begging as outrageous, shameful, degrading to the very name of philosophy and thus to God. This tradition turns that argument on its head. The Cynic is not offensive to God. He is a "friend" of God, *god-like* in his asceticism, and this close and unique relationship is what justifies the practice of begging. The Cynic sage has a *divine right* to ask for alms.

This seems close in spirit to Homer's assertion that the vagabond, especially Odysseus, acts under Zeus's protection and blessing. Indeed, "Diogenes" makes just this connection when he quotes from the *Odyssey* to prove that "the dog is under the protection of the gods and his clothing is god's invention" (Ep. 7). Other letters, however, insist that the Cynic is superior to Odysseus, for Homer's hero begged only occasionally and under duress, not as part of a continuing philosophical or ethical commitment ("Crates" Ep. 19; "Diogenes" Ep. 34).

The idea of a divine right to beg could lead, of course, to terrible abuse, but the Cynic tradition contained, in principle at least, a built-in control for the practice. It is the Cynic *sage* who has a divine right to ask for alms, and the Cynic sage is one who is committed to a life of frugal simplicity. So the Cynic sage may have the right to ask for anything he wishes, but he will not wish for—or ask for—anything more than the bare necessities of life. This idea of Cynic frugality becomes explicit in traditions that directly confront the charge of greed. "Crates," for example, tells his students to beg for the *necessities* of life (Ep. 2). Unscrupulous frauds, he says, beg out of gluttony, but the true Cynic begs only out of hunger and need (Ep. 17). "Diogenes" urges his followers to beg only for things in accord with nature, that is, for simple sustenance like barley meal and not for luxuries that corrupt the soul (Epp. 10, 38).

Repeatedly we have heard the charge that Cynics will beg from anyone, but especially from the gullible, uneducated crowds. The letters are most insistent in denying this. "Crates" thus instructs his students in one of the letters: "Do not beg the necessities of life from everyone. . . . Rather, beg only from those men . . . who have been initiated into philosophy" (Ep. 2). Again and again the warning is sounded: Beg only from the worthy, only from those who are modest or temperate, only from the sage, and not from those who are base, servile, or apathetic ("Crates" Epp. 19, 22, 36; "Diogenes" Ep. 38). Aristotle, of course, had made a similar point about giving only to the "right" people, but these letters are concerned with asking, not with giving.

What do these letters mean when they insist that the Cynic begs only from those initiated into (Cynic) philosophy, only from the (Cynic) sage, only from the (Cynic) worthy? Taken literally, this means that Cynics will beg only from other Cynics. At the very least this would imply that some Cynic sages or initiates possessed more than the bare necessities, thus indicating a moderation of the movement's asceticism. Another implication is more interesting. The Cynic is, by definition, free. He also understands the act of begging as symbolic of a world view and a life-style of self-sufficiency and virtue tied up with simplicity. Thus when these letters claim that Cynics beg only from Cynics, they are insisting that the true Cynic does not ask for alms from just anyone he can persuade or badger into giving. The act of giving must be a free and informed choice based on a bond of mutual understanding and respect. In theory, at least, this places strong limitations on the Cynic practice of begging for alms.

An extension of this idea is that begging should benefit the giver at least as much as the asker-receiver. One letter from "Diogenes" makes this very clear.

> From those who felt gratitude toward me for accepting [what they gave me] the first time, I accepted again as well; but never again from those who did not feel thankful. I scrutinized even the gifts of those who wished to present me barley meal, and accepted it from those who were being benefited. But from the others I took nothing, *since I thought it improper to take something from a person who had himself not received anything [in return]*. (Ep. 38, emphasis added)

The Cynic, then, does not ask something for nothing, but limits his requests to those who understand and benefit from the exchange. How does the giver benefit when asked for money? It is certainly not a question of material benefit, for Cynics scorned material goods. It must be a benefit to the soul.

"Diogenes" seems to address the question when he urges one of his disciples to be bold in begging for alms. It is not at all disgraceful, he says, as long as you are not asking for a free gift (something for nothing) and as long as you do not intend to repay the giver with something of inferior value. It is all right to ask for alms if you do it "for the salvation of everyone," for in that way the Cynic sage is able to give back something much better than he received (Ep. 10).

This is a startling claim. How does the Cynic's begging contribute to the "salvation" of everyone? Cynics had a strong sense of vocation, and their vocation was to serve as "physicians" of the human race, curing men and women of their slavery to material goods and public opinion. Begging was not incidental to this vocation. It illustrated and embodied the nature of the frugal life that leads to self-sufficiency, freedom, and true happiness. This, according to Cynic philosophy, is "salvation." There was, however, also an aggressive aspect to this activity. Begging was not only a way of teaching the path to salvation, it was also a way of *attacking* the attitudes that were enemies of salvation: greed, materialism, and the hypocrisy of popular opinion. All of this is summarized in a letter that "Diogenes" writes to his mother. The Cynic sage begs, he says, to find happiness for himself, to attack false opinions that glorify wealth, to escape the diseases of the marketplace, and to go about the whole earth as one who is "free under father Zeus" (Ep. 34).

Begging, then, is essential to the Cynic's own "salvation." It promotes the "salvation" of others by positive example and negative assault on the enemies of salvation. It allows one to escape the diseases of the marketplace, which seems to be a reference not only to physical diseases but also to the disease which *is* the marketplace with its enslaving emphasis on buying, selling, profits, and greed. And begging contributes to the freedom essential to the Cynic's life-style. The freedom "Diogenes" praises here is the freedom that comes through the renunciation of material goods. Desire for fame and wealth cannot ensnare the Cynic; ties to family and job do not bind him; hardship or a change in fortune cannot affect him. The freedom that begging offers is also, however, a freedom to proclaim the truth boldly. Salaried by no one, indentured to no one, and thus under obligation to no one, the mendicant Cynic is free to act and speak in accordance with his conscience and without fear of economic reprisal.

Conclusions

Our examination of the Cynics was prompted by the desire to gain some degree of understanding of the cultural backdrop of the early Christians' requests for money. It has helped us to see the attitudes toward asking for money in the surrounding culture and to hear at least one group articulate a defense of the practice. It is clear, for example, from the widespread criticism of the Cynics that publicly asking for money was not an approved activity for those who claimed the role of philosopher. This attitude seems to have been well entrenched, for somewhat earlier the Sophists had come in for severe criticism for their practice of teaching rhetoric and philosophy *for a fee*. This is not to say that goods and money did not exchange hands in the philosophical schools, but there was a clear cultural aversion to making an obvious connection between the philosophical life-style and requests for money.

The Cynics, of course, delighted in flouting artificial cultural norms and they embraced begging as a deliberately provocative feature of their style of life. When, however, the movement was sullied by impostors and castigated by critics, the Cynics were forced to define more carefully the principles behind and constraints on their practice of asking for money. These arguments open to us at least a small window on contemporary thinking about the activity of asking for money.

The Cynics viewed begging as acceptable and even necessary since it was an integral part of their mission to save the world. It should therefore illustrate the Cynic's commitment to the life of frugal simplicity; it should be understood as part of the attack on the corrupting power of greed and hypocrisy; and it should contribute to the Cynic's goal of benefiting all humankind. Always the Cynics insisted that asking for alms be free from greed and controlled by frugality. Sometimes they claimed their practice was based on their close relationship with the gods, which was the result of their god-like, ascetic life-style. Sometimes they suggested that they asked in such a way and of such persons that the response to their request was free and informed. Often they insisted that both parties benefit from the exchange, the giver more than the asker-receiver. If the receiver gained modest support for physical necessities, the giver stood to gain salvation.

Lucian described the Cynics' begging as "shearing the sheep." The picture that emerges here, though highly idealized, suggests quite a different picture, with asking and giving taking place within a network of common understanding, mutuality of purpose, and ethical restraint. It should be clear from these letters that the begging of the Cynic philosophers differed in a fundamental way from the practices of the Christian churches, whether ancient or modern. The Cynics were rugged individualists and begged only to satisfy their own frugal needs, not to support a missionary movement or even a local organization. Moreover, it is not clear how much of the Cynic begging was actually influenced by the ideas found in these letters. Yet they provide a context for evaluating the practices of the early Christians.

BENEFACTORS IN GREECE AND ROME

The Cynic letters have provided us with an invaluable window on a group who not only devoted much energy to asking for alms but who also spent time reflecting on this practice. Certainly they were not typical beggars, but the world they inhabited—by choice—was at the lowest end of the economic scale. The money they requested was basically for subsistence, though they imbued the request with additional layers of meaning. At the other end of the economic scale, however, the situation was vastly more complex.

The Burden of Benefaction

This world was inhabited by the wealthy elite, who played the important role of benefactor in Greco-Roman society. Benefactors functioned in many ways in this society. During certain periods they were crucial to the overall economy, making direct donations (called *leitourgias* or "liturgies") to subsidize the food supply, to meet military needs, or to finance public festivals or the construction of public buildings. Alternatively they accepted public offices that involved heavy personal expenditure. Those holding offices involved with the distribution of food, for example, were expected to subsidize the market price, often, A. R. Hands reports, at considerable expense. On a smaller scale benefactors were essential to the vitality of the clubs, guilds, and religious associations so common in that period. A wealthy association member might be asked, for example, to pay for an association dinner or to provide oil for its members' use at the public baths. As on the municipal level, the member might also be elected to an office that involved these financial responsibilities.

Though ostensibly voluntary, these benefactions, especially those on the public level, became almost a regular form of taxation. As such they were increasingly burdensome and potentially ruinous to the well-to-do. Aristotle, for example, assumed that the health of the political structure depended on the generosity of the wealthy, but he warned that they should not be bled dry: "It is better to prevent men from undertaking costly but useless public services like equipping choruses and torch races and all other similar services" (*Politics* 5.7.11). Isocrates, an older contemporary of Aristotle, complained that "it has become far more dangerous to be suspected of being well off than to be detected in crime; for criminals are pardoned or let off with slight penalties, while the rich are ruined utterly" by repeated requests for benefactions (*Antidosis* 160). Somewhat closer to the New Testament period, Cicero insisted that "the whole system of public bounties in such extravagant amount is intrinsically wrong; but," he goes on to say, "it may under certain circumstances be necessary to make them" (*On Duties* 2.17.60).

Prompting the Benefaction

Cicero's last comment raises the question that is of interest to us here. What were the circumstances that prompted asking and encouraging giving? On both the municipal level and the level of smaller associations, the wealthy were called upon to finance many of the expenses. On what grounds were the requests made? What motivated the wealthy to give? We do not have copies of the original requests; the sources of our information here are primarily the many inscriptions in which the recipients of these benefactions recorded their gratitude on stone or marble stelae. We must work backward from these to try to determine the cultural patterns that controlled requests for money at this level of society.

Certainly patriotism or community spirit played a strong motivating role. Inscriptions repeatedly praise the zeal and loyalty of the benefactors as well as their philanthropy and public spirit. Another factor that is repeatedly documented is the benefactor's desire for honor and glory. In fact, a number of inscriptions appeal to this sentiment to motivate additional gifts. The people of Miletos, for example, inscribed not only the various honors granted to a benefactor but also the purpose of the inscription: "so that others also might make it their policy to be concerned about the temple in Didyma and about the People of Miletos, as they observe the benefactors of the temple being honored by the People." A frequent device to encourage more generous giving was carefully to grade the honors and titles according to the size of the benefaction. (This technique has proved enduringly successful. Recently my alma mater, whose mascot is the owl, offered me the opportunity to become a member of the Diamond Owls, the Platinum Owls, the Golden Owls, the Silver Owls, or, several steps lower and at rock bottom, the Hoot Owls, depending on the size of my contribution to the Booster Club.)

Inherent in this practice of bestowing honors and especially of grading them is the crucial idea of the reciprocity of gift-giving. Every gift demands a counter-gift. This concept influences our actions even today, but it was much more explicit and formal in the ancient world. The recipient of a gift was placed under obligation to respond with a gift of at least equal value, and pride usually required the return of a superior gift instead. The superior return gift then placed the original donor under obligation to respond with an even larger gift, and the cycle continued. In this situation, then, the bestowal of honors on a benefactor was not simply an act of gratitude. It was viewed by both parties as the equivalent of the expected return gift. Indeed, the honors were intended to surpass the original gift in worth and thus to stimulate a further round of benefaction. A request for a benefaction was thus not made in a vacuum. It presupposed and created a network of obligations that bound asker and giver, donor and recipient, in a continuing relationship. In Roman society this was formalized as the patron (donor) and client (receiver) relationship, which formed a bond equivalent to that of the extended family.

Not every benefaction, of course, was stimulated by the noble concept of reciprocity. Honors were cheap and the resources of benefactors, though great, were not unlimited. Thus gifts were often demanded and made under pressure—the pressure of public opinion or the fear of an uprising by the people, who came to expect benefactions like subsidized grain or public games as their right. Occasionally the pressure was outright extortion. When, for example, appeals were made for special collections or subscription funds, lists of people who agreed to participate were often published, as well as lists of those who had agreed to contribute money and then failed to do so. The motive here has shifted from honoring contributors to publicly shaming noncontributors. When Cicero, in the quotation above, mentioned certain circumstances where bounties (benefactions) may be necessary, he was referring to just this situation of public pressure. Capitulation to the demands of the populace for a benefaction was sometimes an expedient way to obtain public office or to avoid public embarrassment. "If, therefore, such entertainment is demanded by the people, men of right judgment must at least consent to furnish it, *even if they do not like the idea*" (*On Duties* 2.17.58).

Conclusions

The practice of benefaction, which involved implicit or explicit requests for large-scale gifts of money, sustained the Greco-Roman world at several levels. It was an accepted practice with roots deep in the notion of the reciprocity of gift-giving, yet problems were apparent to those caught up in the process. To be sure, these problems need to be evaluated in the light of the unequal distribution of wealth in the Greco-Roman world, but that goes far beyond our purposes here. It is clear that within the system of benefaction—and especially from the perspective of the benefactors—the requests could get out of hand. Requests became expectations, expectations became demands, and demands were accompanied by thinly veiled threats. The voluntary quality of the benefaction was thus seriously compromised.

On the positive side, the ancient system of benefaction highlights the concept of reciprocity inherent in gift-giving and implicit in all requests for gifts. The Cynic letters alluded to this, as when "Diogenes" insisted that it is "improper to take something from a person who had not himself received anything." In the practice of benefaction, however, the sense of the mutual and continuing obligation established by the giving and receiving of gifts emerges as a strong factor in every request for money.

FOR FURTHER READING

Many books on ancient philosophy ignore the Cynics or dismiss them in a few pages. Samuel Dill, however, has a fine chapter on Cynicism in his book, *Roman Society from Nero to Marcus Aurelius* (New York: Meridian, 1956 [first published in 1904]), and J. M. Rist's chapter on Cynicism in his *Stoic Philosophy* (Cambridge: Cambridge University Press, 1969) is very helpful. Donald R. Dudley gives the subject a very thorough treatment in his book, *A History of Cynicism* (London: Methuen, 1937), though it has been criticized as somewhat inaccurate and may be too technical for most readers. Abraham J. Malherbe's article, "Cynics," in the Supplementary Volume of *The Interpreter's Dictionary of the Bible* (Nashville: Abingdon, 1976) provides a concise and reliable introduction to these philosophers.

In this chapter I have referred several times to A. R. Hands, whose book, *Charities and Social Aid in Greece and Rome* (Ithaca, N.Y.: Cornell University Press, 1968) provides a learned and readable survey of attitudes toward giving and toward the poor in the ancient world. *The Gift* by Marcel Mauss (Glencoe, Ill.: Free Press, 1954) provides a provocative analysis of the ritual aspect of gift-giving. Mauss focuses primarily on anthropological data from Polynesia, Melanesia, and Northwest America, but his conclusions shed light on the phenomenon in the Greco-Roman world. Raw data for the benefactor theme have been collected by Frederick W. Danker in *Benefactor* (St. Louis, Mo.: Clayton, 1982), but Hands's analysis of the motif in chapters 3 and 4 of his book is probably more helpful for the general reader. I should also mention M. I. Finley, whose book, *The World of Odysseus* (New York: Viking Press, 1965), provides a clear introduction to the social world evoked by Homer's epic.

I have quoted from a number of Greek and Roman writers using the translations in The Loeb Classical Library (Cambridge, Mass.: Harvard University Press). Aristotle's *Nicomachean Ethics* (1926) and *Politics* (1932) were translated by H. Rackham. Cicero's *On Duties* (*De Officiis*) was translated by Walter Miller (1913), and Seneca's essays "On the Happy Life" and "On Benefits" were translated by John W. Basore in *Moral Essays,* vol. 2 (1932) and vol. 3 (1935) respectively. Lucian's two essays, "The Fisherman" and "The Runaways," are found in vol. 3 (1921) and vol. 5 (1936) of his collected essays, translated for Loeb by A. M. Harmon. They should be read in their entirety to sense the depth of animosity stirred up by degenerate Cynic beggars. Dio Chrysostom's oration is found in *Discourses,* vol. 3, translated by J. W. Cohoon and H. Lamar Crosby (1940); Isocrates' oration was translated by George Norlin (1929). Book 6 of *Lives of Eminent Philosophers* by Diogenes Laertius, translated by R. D. Hicks (1925), is devoted to the Cynics. It is an interesting but uncritical and anecdotal report of their lives, highlighting their outlandish behavior. Epictetus's essay, on the other hand, describes the ideal Cynic and focuses on the ethical goals of the movement; it is found in *Discourses,* vol. 2, translated by W. A. Oldfather (1928). Finally, the Cynic letters have been cited from Abraham J. Malherbe's *Cynic Epistles* (Missoula, Mont.: Scholars Press, 1977).

CHAPTER 2

PERSPECTIVES FROM THE GOSPELS: RADICAL POVERTY

Take nothing for your journey, no staff,
nor bag, nor bread, nor money.
—*Luke* 9:3

T he natural starting point for investigating what the New Testament has to say about the practice of asking for money is the gospels. Yet at this very point we run into difficulties. First, the evidence is slim and difficult to interpret. The gospels record many sayings about poverty and riches, tithing and almsgiving, but very few directly related to the issue that interests us here: *asking* for money. In fact, the question of asking for financial support emerges at only one point in the gospels: Jesus' instructions to his disciples when he sends them away on a preaching and healing mission of their own. Here, though, we confront a second problem.

The gospels were written decades after the events they describe and each was written for a different community. This means that in the years immediately following Jesus' ministry, the stories about him were handed down orally and only gradually collected and fixed in writing. Oral forms are inherently flexible, so it is likely that during this period the traditions were shaped by the needs and experiences of the groups that used them. Even when these traditions were written down, the situations of the communities for which they were written had an impact on what was remembered about Jesus and how it was remembered. Thus the mission instructions to the disciples are preserved for us in four versions which, though very similar, are not identical (Matt.

10:5-15; Mark 6:8-11; Luke 9:3-5; and Luke 10:2-12). We must look carefully at the various renderings of these instructions and consider their implications for the practice of asking for money. We will need to ask the following questions of each gospel: How were the disciples instructed to support themselves while proclaiming the gospel? What was the historical and theological significance of these instructions?

The radical quality of the mission instructions, quoted above in their Lukan form, is immediately obvious, and this raises another question. How long did the early Christians actually follow these rigorous practices? The gospels suggest different answers. Luke, for example, shows a keen interest in Jesus' mission instructions, but, as we will see, he is also careful to show that the practices demanded of the followers of the earthly Jesus do not hold for later generations. Yet the Gospel of Matthew, written near the end of the first century, seems to suggest that an ascetic movement of itinerant "prophets" was still actively following the instructions at that time. The *Didache*, or *Teaching of the Twelve Apostles*, a Christian document written at the end of the first century, confirms the existence of this movement. The missionary zeal of the early Christians is not to be doubted. The question of how they supported this activity is, however, a complex one, and the gospels provide an ambiguous picture. We thus need to begin our investigation with the period before the gospels were written. Of course, we can only make educated guesses about the early shape and significance of the mission instructions. Yet we need to gain as clear a picture as possible about this period, for only then will we be able to understand the significance of the various developments we can see in the written gospels.

BEHIND THE CONFLICTING INSTRUCTIONS: RADICAL TRUST

The first three gospels—Matthew, Mark, and Luke—relate that after Jesus singled out twelve of his disciples to form a special group, he sent them on a preaching and healing mission to the surrounding towns and villages. Nothing is said about the precise location or duration of this mission and little is said about its results. Mark and Luke, for example, report the mission's success in only the most general terms (Mark 6:12-13; Luke 9:6), while Matthew does not even do that. All three, however, present in somewhat surprising detail Jesus' instructions on what the disciples were to wear and carry on their trip and how they were to find lodging. These instructions were obviously considered important, since they were preserved when other aspects of the mission were not, yet the three gospels disagree on their content.

In Mark 6:8-11, Jesus says that the disciples are to take "nothing" for the journey: no bread, no bag (for provisions), no money, and no extra clothing. Two exceptions are noted: They may take a staff and wear sandals. When they come to a village they are to accept the hospitality of the first house that offers it and remain there until they leave that village. Instructions are given for dealing with places that refuse to extend any hospitality. Matthew's gospel includes a number of instructions not found in Mark and presents the prohibitions in a different sequence (Matt. 10:5-15). The prohibitions are also more rigorous. As in Mark, the disciples are to take no money, bag, or extra garment. Unlike Mark, though, they are also denied the use of sandals and staff. No mention is made of bread. The instructions for locating suitable lodging are more detailed but similar in content. Luke's version is closer to Matthew's than to Mark's in the rigor of its prohibitions: no staff, no bag, no bread, no money, and no second garment (Luke 9:3-5). Luke does not mention sandals in the mission of the twelve. In the next chapter, though, he describes another mission not found in the other gospels, the mission of the seventy (10:1-20). These are instructed not to wear sandals or to take a bag for provisions or a purse for money. Like the twelve, they are to stay in the first house that offers them lodging. There is thus a core of common instructions (no money, no bag for provisions, and no changing of lodging), disagreement on others (staff and sandals), and some items (bread, garments, sandals, and staff) are missing from some lists.

The flexibility of the period of oral transmission and the theological concerns of the different evangelists have produced these variations, and it is impossible, given the disagreement on so many details, to determine precisely the original content of the instructions. We can distinguish, however, two basic forms: a "rigorous" form reflected in Matthew and Luke and a "relaxed" form (permitting sandals and staff) found in Mark. The question is, which represents the earliest form? Where should we begin our investigation? Though Mark is widely recognized as the oldest gospel, and though it probably served as a source for Matthew and Luke, one cannot always assume that it contains the oldest version of a tradition. Matthew and Luke had access to written and oral material independent of Mark, and some of it was at least as old as Mark. In the case of the mission instructions, it is the general consensus among scholars that the more rigorous form is older.

Scholars have reconstructed the rigorous version of the mission instructions used by Matthew and Luke. In it the disciples were told to take "nothing" for their journey: no bag, no money, no second garment, no staff, and no sandals. They were to rely on the hospitality of the people to whom they preached, staying where they were welcomed and eating and drinking whatever was provided. If a village refused them hospitality, they were to respond by shaking the dust of its streets from their feet.

Though these instructions probably came to Matthew and Luke as part of a written document, they were transmitted in oral form before they were put in writing. It is really that period and that form of the instructions that we are interested in. The reason for this is fairly simple. It is probable that these instructions were preserved by a group that lived by their demands, for the instructions would not have been remembered in such detail if they had not been put into practice. Yet the life-style suggested by the instructions does not permit the luxury of writing materials: no bag, no money, no second garment—and certainly no quill pens and parchment. So it is in the period of *oral* transmission that the demands of the instructions could be met by the life-style of the participants. Yet it is difficult enough to reconstruct the written version used by Matthew and Luke; to determine the exact shape and content of the oral instructions is impossible. We can only assume—and hope—that the oral tradition was not much different from the early written version that has been reconstructed. We need to imagine, then, in the first decades after Easter, a group of itinerant preachers who lived a life of radical poverty as they moved about the Palestinian countryside proclaiming Jesus' message of the kingdom. They carried no provisions and relied entirely on the hospitality of villagers for support. What was the social and theological significance of the mission instructions for this group? How did they ask for support?

The first thing that strikes one is the radical, illogical quality of these instructions. All the normal preparations for a journey, even the most basic equipment of staff and sandals, are prohibited. Why? Gerd Theissen, a New Testament scholar who has investigated the nature of early Palestinian Christianity, argues that one purpose of the prohibitions was to distinguish the missionaries from the Cynic beggars, whose typical equipment included coat, staff, and bag. "It is clear," Theissen says, "that the usual practices of [Cynic] beggars were forbidden to the early itinerant Christian charismatics." But a staff for protection, a bag for provisions, a second garment for cover at night, money, and especially sandals were the equipment of *any* foot-traveler in rural Palestine, while Cynic beggars were probably not a common feature of that region. Thus the original purpose of the instructions was probably not to distinguish Christian missionaries from Cynic beggars but to set them apart from all other travelers and to convey through their striking mode

41

of dress and travel a theological message. To appreciate fully the theological significance of these instructions, they need to be read in conjunction with other sayings that probably derive from the same social and theological environment.

One cluster of sayings that may have circulated with the mission instructions proclaims, for example, the radical demands of discipleship:

> As they were going along the road, someone said to him, "I will follow you wherever you go." And Jesus said to him, "Foxes have holes, and birds of the air have nests; but the Son of Man has nowhere to lay his head." To another he said, "Follow me." But he said, "Lord, first let me go and bury my father." But Jesus said to him, "Let the dead bury their own dead; but as for you, go and proclaim the kingdom of God." Another said, "I will follow you, Lord; but let me first say farewell to those at my home." Jesus said to him, "No one who puts a hand to the plow and looks back is fit for the kingdom of God." (Luke 9:57-62; *see also* Matt. 8:19-22)

Would-be disciples are asked to sacrifice the comforts and security of home, family, and possessions in order to proclaim the kingdom. Here is an ethos of rootlessness, homelessness, and total commitment similar to that of the mission instructions. What theological vision sustained such radical demands? Jesus' words on anxiety, also preserved in Matthew and Luke, suggest the answer:

> Therefore I tell you, do not worry about your life, what you will eat, or about your body, what you will wear. For life is more than food, and the body more than clothing. Consider the ravens: they neither sow nor reap, they have neither storehouse nor barn, and yet God feeds them. Of how much more value are you than the birds! And can any of you by worrying add a single hour to your span of life? If then you are not able to do so small a thing as that, why do you worry about the rest? Consider the lilies, how they grow: they neither toil nor spin; yet I tell you, even Solomon in all his

glory was not clothed like one of these. But if God so clothes the grass of the field, which is alive today and tomorrow is thrown into the oven, how much more will he clothe you—you of little faith! And do not keep striving for what you are to eat and what you are to drink, and do not keep worrying. For it is the nations of the world that strive after all these things, and your Father knows that you need them. Instead, strive for his kingdom, and these things will be given to you as well. (Luke 12:22-31; *see also* Matt. 6:25-33)

In the instructions for the mission, the disciples are asked to live out this message of radical trust: God will provide. In the way they conducted their mission, the disciples were to exemplify a trust in God so profound that the most basic preparations for a journey were unnecessary. No hint of self-sufficiency was permitted, nor was it needed: God would work through the hospitality of the villagers to sustain those sent to proclaim the message of the kingdom. Clearly this has important implications for the practice of asking for money.

Theissen, who sees Cynic begging as the background of this material, suggests that the instructions were promoting an alternative mode of begging, one that he calls "charismatic." He uses this word in a technical sense to indicate that the mode of life was not an institutionalized one but was grounded in "a call over which [the charismatic] had no control." Theissen concludes that the life-style of the mission "was certainly no ordinary mendicancy but charismatic begging which trusted in God to sustain his missionaries." He has rightly captured the element of trust implicit in the instructions, but the reference to "charismatic begging" seems to me to misplace their emphasis. There is no indication that the mission instructions ever mentioned the practice of begging. They do not advocate *asking* for money or food or shelter. Instead we find only the confident expectation that the missionaries' message would evoke in some villagers a positive response that would result in an offer of food and shelter. The instructions thus encouraged charismatic *trust* on the part of the messengers of the kingdom and presupposed as well a charismatic *hospitality* on the part of the villagers. Indeed, the spontaneous hospitality of the villagers was as much a sign of the kingdom as the radical poverty of the messengers. It signified trust in the messengers and acceptance of their message that the kingdom of God had drawn near. If an expression of need was part of the exchange with the villagers, and we have no proof that it was, it may have been used as a test of a villager's receptivity to the message of the kingdom. Matthew and Mark, at least, present the two acts of receiving the messengers and the message as if they were one: "If anyone will not welcome you or listen to your words . . ." (Matt. 10:14; *see also* Mark 6:11).

This message of the nearness of the kingdom was an important aspect of the missionary movement. Matthew and Luke cite it to summarize the content of the mission preaching: "The kingdom of heaven has come near" (Matt. 10:7); "The kingdom of God has come near to you" (Luke 10:9, 11). Elsewhere Matthew is even more explicit: "Truly I tell you, you will not have gone through all the towns of Israel before the Son of Man comes" (Matt. 10:23). This message seems to characterize the early period of the mission movement and indicates that the adherents of this movement went forth with the expectation of the imminent return of the Son of Man. Thus the mission instructions not only advocated radical trust, they also presupposed a movement of short duration.

Any group, then, that lived the spirit as well as the letter of these instructions would journey forth with some urgency to proclaim the message of the kingdom. There was to be no thought of self-protection or self-support, only radical trust in God to provide all that was necessary until the full advent of the kingdom. This provision would come in the form of hospitality from the villagers, and it was to be accepted without question, without complaint, and certainly without requests for more. Asking for support may have occurred. It may even have been used as a test of the villagers, much as Elijah tested the widow of Zarephath (I Kings 17:8-16). Nevertheless, it stood in some tension with the ethos of the movement and certainly it was not the movement's defining trait.

As time passed a number of changes occurred that affected mission practices. The delay in the arrival of the kingdom, for example, altered somewhat the ethos of the movement. The development of stable Christian communities constituted another important change, for these communities could now be counted on to support the traveling mission workers. The work was thus less risky but also more profitable, and corruption emerged within the movement, bringing other changes in its wake. We see evidence of these changes in the way the gospels preserved the mission instructions. A non-canonical document from about the same time period, the *Didache*, provides even clearer evidence of change. We will thus look at this document before considering the canonical gospels.

THE *DIDACHE:* SIGNS OF ABUSE

The *Didache*, written in Syria at the end of the first century or the beginning of the second, gives us a picture of the radical itinerancy movement at this later period. Circumstances have changed. No longer were the itinerant messengers always advancing into new "unchurched" territory. More and more they were encountering established churches, and this changed considerably the dynamics of the interaction between messenger and community. Furthermore, the *Didache* discusses this interaction from the perspective of the host communities, whose concerns were different from those of the itinerant messengers. We find in this document, for example, instructions on how to respond to visiting missionaries, not on how to conduct a missionary journey. In particular, it is evident from the instructions that the original program of trust and hospitality had been somewhat abused, and this has left its mark on the attitude of the Christian communities.

The *Didache* opens with a description of the "Two Ways, one of Life and one of Death." This material may have been taken over from an earlier, pre-Christian source, but the experiences of the Syrian Christians have certainly shaped the selection and presentation of the material. The foremost precept of the Way of Life is the Great Commandment: "First, thou shalt love the God who made thee, secondly, thy neighbor as thyself" (*Did.* 1.2). The document then explains what it means to love the neighbor, and that includes the practice of almsgiving: "Give to everyone that asks thee, and do not refuse, for the Father's will is that we give to all from the gifts we have received" (1.5). Yet this encouragement of generosity is immediately qualified by extensive warnings against those who would abuse it:

> Woe to him who receives; for if any man receive alms under pressure of need he is innocent; but he who receives it without need shall be tried as to why he took and for what, and being in prison he shall be examined as to his deeds, and "he shall not come out thence until he pay the last farthing." But concerning this it was also said, "Let thine alms sweat into thine hands *until thou knowest to whom thou art giving*." (*Did.* 1.5-6, emphasis added)

This wary attitude, surely born of painful experience, also colors the later instructions concerning the reception of itinerant "apostles and prophets," who appeared at the doors of the church expecting support. The document first admonishes the Christians to receive these travelers and even to tolerate any unusual liturgical practices they might have: "But suffer the prophets to hold Eucharist as they will" (10.7). The travelers' needs were to be met with hospitality, though this hospitality has lost its spontaneous quality and has become instead a church mandate. Thus the *Didache* instructs the churches to support the prophets for a few days and to provide them with a day's ration of bread when they leave.

This mandated hospitality, however, was subject to widespread abuse and the *Didache* urges precautions to protect against this. First a doctrinal test was established: "Whosoever then comes and teaches you all these things aforesaid, receive him. But if the teacher himself be perverted and teach another doctrine to destroy these things, do not listen to him" (11.1-2). Next a time limit was set on the visiting preachers: "Let him not stay more than one day, or if need be a second as well; but if he stay three days, he is a false prophet" (11.5). The church was also instructed to look carefully for any evidence of greed: "If he ask for money, he is a false prophet" (11.6). They were to be particularly wary of those who misused spiritual gifts for personal gain: "No prophet who orders a meal in a spirit shall eat of it: otherwise he is a false prophet" (11.9). "Whosoever shall say in a spirit 'Give me money, or something else,' you shall not listen to him; but if he tell you to give on behalf of others in want, let none judge him" (11.12).

The phenomenon of itinerant messengers thus seems to have endured in Syria into the second century. Though written from a different perspective, the *Didache* presents a picture that complements in many ways the early mission instructions. There is no mention of sandals, staff, or garments, but the comments in the *Didache* clearly presuppose charismatic messengers traveling without provisions. Yet significant changes are evident. The movement was in a transitional period, and wandering prophets and settled communities coexisted rather uneasily. Because spontaneous hospitality had been replaced by a mandated form, the element of radical trust that characterized the original movement was gone. Moreover, there is evidence of corruption in the movement and a correspondingly wary attitude on the part of the community. Thus the *Didache* is not interested in whether the prophet trusts radically in God but in whether the prophet is worthy of the church's hospitality. In this situation requests for money were very significant, for they revealed the true nature of a prophet. If made for personal gain, the request was a sign of a false prophet; if made on behalf of the needy, it confirmed a true one. The significance of asking for money has thus been completely transformed. Earlier it was not a prominent aspect of the instructions to the itinerant workers, though it may have served as a test of the response of the villages. Here it is far more prominent and it has become the community's way of testing the prophets.

The gospels, by incorporating the mission instructions into their narratives, transform the message in other more subtle ways. We turn now to consider the instructions within their gospel settings.

SHIFTING EMPHASES WITHIN THE GOSPELS

We have looked at the mission instructions in the form and setting in which they first circulated and have seen evidence of greed corrupting the movement and establishing the illicitness of asking for money. Now we need to consider these instructions within the literary and theological settings provided by the gospels. Each time these instructions were incorporated by an evangelist into his gospel, they became part of a larger narrative and a wider theological pattern. Through slight changes in wording, sequence, and context, they acquired different emphases and new layers of meaning, corresponding to some extent with the changed interests and circumstances of the evangelists and their communities. In particular, the significance of asking for money changed slightly in these three gospels, and we need to note and discuss these changes. We begin with Matthew.

Matthew

Matthew presents a picture of radical itinerant ministry that is similar in many ways to that of the *Didache*. Both documents were written in the late first century and both derive from the area of Syria-Palestine. Both were aware of itinerant missionaries and both were concerned with mercenary motives that were corrupting the movement. But whereas in the *Didache* the evidence comes from explicit directives to the church, in Matthew the evidence is found in the way the mission instructions are presented. These instructions are part of a considerably longer speech on mission concerns (Matt. 10:5-42) and contain sayings either not found in the other gospels or found there in different contexts. The instructions open, for example, with the admonition to "go nowhere among the Gentiles" (10:5). The disciples are told what message to preach and what activities to perform. Then they are given the following charge: "You received without payment; give without payment" (v. 8). This charge is found only in Matthew's gospel and it establishes remuneration—or the renunciation of it—as a primary concern of this evangelist. The familiar mission instructions that follow are presented in a way that continues to emphasize this concern about recompense.

Whereas Mark and Luke refer to staff, bread, and bag before mentioning money, Matthew's instructions refer to money first, thereby giving priority to this particular concern. Matthew increases the emphasis on money even more by including in the command all possible forms of coinage: "Take no gold, or silver, or copper in your belts." There is also a significant change in the verb of command, though the New Revised Standard Version's translation obscures this. Mark and Luke prohibit the twelve from "taking" money *with them* on the journey, but Matthew uses a verb that suggests more the action of "acquiring" money. The effect of all of this is that Matthew's gospel speaks not so much about preparations for the mission journey as it does about seeking payment while on it. Edgar J. Goodspeed's translation captures best this nuance of the text: "Give without payment, just as you received without payment. Do not accept gold or silver or copper money to put in your pockets" (10:8-9).

The rest of the instructions follow the rigorous form (both staff and sandals are prohibited), and they close with the comment that "laborers deserve their food" (v. 10). This then provides the explicit reason for refusing remuneration and renouncing normal travel arrangements: The missionary workers will be provided with food. Matthew does not give any indication of how this will occur, though he is more specific on the issue of lodging: "Whatever town or village you enter, find out who in it is worthy, and stay there until you leave" (v. 11). The search for someone who is "worthy" suggests something different from the spontaneous hospitality that seemed to support the mission in its earliest period. It may point to an organized system, and if that is the case then Matthew is close to the *Didache* on this point also. Yet hospitality is still regarded as a sign of openness to the message, and those who refuse to extend it are subject to an ominous action that anticipates the coming judgment:

> If anyone will not welcome you or listen to your words, shake off the dust from your feet as you leave that house or town. Truly I tell you, it will be more tolerable for the land of Sodom and Gomorrah on the day of judgment than for that town.
> (vv. 14-15)

The sayings collected in the rest of the chapter emphasize the hardships the disciples can expect to face, and the rigorous mission instructions are consistent with this theme. Matthew does not record the results of the mission; he does not even report the disciples' return. At the end of the gospel, however, he does report a second mission charge by the resurrected Jesus that partially supplants and partially reinforces the earlier one (28:18-20). In these instructions the earlier restriction limiting the mission to Israel is lifted and the disciples are now directed to go to "all nations." Nothing more is said, however, about journey preparations or financial support. Have these restrictions been lifted also? It would seem that this is *not* the case, for these final instructions continue with the charge to teach "everything that I have commanded you," and that would include the earlier instructions on how to conduct a mission. Matthew thus presupposes a continuation of the radical demands of itinerancy but with an extension of the mission to the Gentiles. Other passages in the gospel confirm that Matthew's community was not only familiar with radical itinerancy but was also aware of abuses in the movement.

Alone of all the gospels, Matthew speaks explicitly of the reward that awaits those who receive a "prophet" or a "righteous person." The evangelist does not explain who these people are, but it is not hard to see the phenomenon of radical itinerancy behind these words:

> Whoever welcomes a prophet in the name of a prophet will receive a prophet's reward; and whoever welcomes a righteous person in the name of a righteous person will receive the reward of the righteous; and whoever gives even a cup of cold water to one of these little ones in the name of a disciple—truly I tell you, none of these will lose their reward.
> (10:41-42)

In another passage unique to Matthew, hospitality is described as the sole criterion of the final judgment (25:31-46). This confirms in a rather striking way the words in the mission instructions concerning the fate of those who refuse to receive the messengers of the kingdom.

If these texts reflect a contemporary concern in Matthew's community with the reception of itinerant prophets, others convey a concern about those who abuse this role. One saying found only in this gospel warns about "false prophets, who come to you in sheep's clothing but inwardly are ravenous wolves" (7:15). The text clearly has traveling prophets in mind and their characterization as "ravenous wolves" suggests greed. The focus on recompense that we have seen in the mission instructions completes the picture of abuse.

Like the other gospels, Matthew was written for a particular Christian community. All the information in the gospel, though deriving from an earlier period, was filtered through the experience of that community. Matthew's distinctive focus on hospitality and wandering prophets thus points to a continuing involvement with an itinerant movement. As in the *Didache*, corruption of this movement has generated a particular concern for the question of remuneration. Through the instructions to the disciples, Matthew's church was given a missionary model that was also a warning against the mercenary motives of the false prophets. "You will know them by their fruits" (7:16), and asking for money was viewed in this church as a sure sign of corrupt fruit.

Mark

If Matthew attests to considerable interest in the radical prophetic movement at the turn of the century in Syria, Mark, written somewhat earlier and perhaps for a Roman community, presents a rather different picture. The most obvious difference in Mark's gospel is that the mission instructions are given in a "relaxed" form: "He ordered them to take nothing for their journey *except a staff;* no bread, no bag, no money in their belts; *but to wear sandals* and not to put on two tunics" (Mark 6:8-9, emphases added). As we noted earlier, it is generally agreed that the rigorous form of the mission instructions is older and the exceptions in Mark's account are a secondary development. It is impossible, however, to determine whether Mark knew the tradition in the more rigorous form and modified it or whether the tradition came to him in this modified version. Whatever their origin, Mark's instructions still require that journey preparations be kept to a minimum. The disciples are to take no provisions, no bag for provisions, and no money to buy provisions. On the other hand, a staff for protection and sandals for the feet—the most elementary equipment for an overland trip—are not only permitted but required. Indeed, it is a bit surprising that these two items are mentioned, much less required, since without any instructions to the contrary they would be a natural part of the traveler's equipment. The effect, however, of explicitly instructing the disciples to take a staff and to wear sandals on their feet is to call attention to these items. An alert reader might then recall that the people of Israel were given the same instructions on the eve of their flight from Egypt.

According to the book of Exodus, after the first nine plagues had been leveled against Pharaoh and Egypt, with no evidence of a softening of Pharaoh's "hardened" heart, God announced the tenth and final plague: the death of all the first-born in the land of Egypt. At the same time God gave instructions to Israel for a special "passover" ritual that would allow them to escape this plague. God also directed them to prepare for a hasty flight from Egypt:

> This is how you shall eat [the passover lamb]: your loins girded, your sandals on your feet, and your staff in your hand; and you shall eat it hurriedly. It is the passover of the Lord. For I will pass through the land of Egypt that night, and I will strike down every firstborn in the land of Egypt, both human beings and animals; on all the gods of Egypt I will execute judgments: I am the Lord. (Exod. 12:11-12)

By echoing this tradition, Mark's instructions present an image of standing, as Israel had, on the very threshold of God's decisive act of redemption. This underscores the tone of urgency that was part of the early mission instructions, but this sense of urgency is not limited in Mark to these instructions. It is a thematic motif of the entire gospel.

The rest of the mission instructions are presented very briefly. They lack many of the details in Matthew and Luke about finding lodging, and without these details the instructions hardly make sense. The treatment of the villages that do not extend hospitality is somewhat more benign. The action of shaking dust off the feet is recommended, but the meaning of the action is not given nor are the villages threatened with the fate of Sodom and Gomorrah.

The implications of these instructions for the practice of asking for money are not drawn out. Unlike Matthew, asking for money is not explicitly mentioned or implicitly highlighted by the narrative. Certainly there is no evidence of concern about fraud and not much concern with presenting the instructions in a useful form. Indeed, nothing indicates that Mark had a special historical interest in itinerant missionaries or their means of subsistence. This may imply that radical itinerancy did not play a significant role in Mark's community.

Luke

When we turn to Luke's mission instructions we find something quite different from either Matthew or Mark. Not only did this evangelist highlight the mission instructions more than the others, but when he wrote the book of Acts he was able to illustrate these instructions through concrete examples in the story of the early church. In a more significant vein, this gospel shows the dramatic changes that occurred when the Christian mission moved from rural Palestine and Syria to the urban centers of the Roman Empire. The original mission instructions were no longer relevant. If Mark suggested this by his disinterest, Luke took a more direct approach.

At first Luke gives a very terse report of the mission instructions to the twelve. The pattern is familiar. They are sent out to preach the kingdom of God and to heal (Luke 9:2). They are charged to take nothing for the journey (v. 3) and told how to respond to an inhospitable reception (v. 5). They depart (v. 6) and on their return report what they have done (v. 10). Initially nothing suggests any special interest in the episode. In the next chapter, however, Luke describes a second mission, which is not found in any of the other gospels (10:1-20). Seventy (or seventy-two) *others* are sent out on a mission very similar to that of the twelve, but here the instructions are presented in more detail. Even the return of the seventy is described with a depth of enthusiasm not found in the earlier report: "The seventy returned with joy, saying, 'Lord, in your name even the demons submit to us!' He said to them, 'I watched Satan fall from heaven like a flash of lightning'" (10:17-18). Furthermore, the seventy are instructed to pray for even more workers to send into the harvest (v. 2). Luke's message seems clear: The mission that extends Jesus' ministry into new territory is not limited to the original twelve. Others will participate and even overshadow the work of the twelve. The continuation of the story in Acts confirms this, for first Stephen (Acts 6:8–7:53), then Philip (8:4-40), and finally Paul and Barnabas (9:1–28:31) are shown carrying the message of Jesus into the heart of the Roman Empire while the twelve gradually fade from sight.

According to Luke 10, this new mission should rest on the same elements of trust and hospitality that characterized the earlier mission of the twelve: "Carry no purse, no bag, no sandals" (v. 4). Yet there are subtle changes. Neither the context nor the content of the instructions to the twelve suggests great danger. In the instructions to the seventy, however, Luke highlights the element of danger by opening with the words, "Go on your way. See, I am sending you out like lambs into the midst of wolves" (v. 3). Luke also does not forbid the seventy to carry staffs. Staffs were used for protection. Does this tacit permission to carry a staff signal an accommodation to changing circumstances? An even greater change is signaled by the fact that now, for the first time, there is approval of wages for the messengers (v. 7). To be sure, these wages are defined in terms of the hospitality they receive, but hospitality is now regarded as the messenger's right. This changes the financial arrangements considerably. Hospitality is no longer viewed as a vehicle for God's providential care but as the wages due the messengers for the services they have rendered.

These hints of change, however, simply foreshadow a radical development that occurs in a conversation that Luke (and *only* Luke) reports between Jesus and his disciples at the Last Supper:

> He said to them, "When I sent you out without a purse, bag, or sandals, did you lack anything?" They said, "No, not a thing." He said to them, "But now, the one who has a purse must take it, and likewise a bag. And the one who has no sword must sell his cloak and buy one." . . . They said, "Lord, look, here are two swords." He replied, "It is enough."
> (22:35-38)

With these words Jesus emphatically annuls the peculiar instructions that have given the disciples' mission its distinctive theological significance. Luke seems aware that the circumstances that permitted conducting the mission with an attitude of radical trust have passed. The mission itself is not thereby annulled. It is to continue after Jesus' death. But from now on the disciples are to carry a purse and bag, and they are to receive a wage. They are even to prepare for hostile circumstances, though the significance of Jesus' abrupt reaction to the two swords ("It is enough") remains an enigma. Again Acts confirms this message, for it describes Peter, Stephen, Paul, and other Christian messengers repeatedly facing hostile crowds, prison, and even death. And Paul's extensive travels, as we will see in the next chapter, required careful financial arrangements.

CONCLUSIONS

We began our survey of the practice of asking for money with the mission instructions of early Palestinian Christianity. Since this period left no written documents, these early instructions had to be reconstructed from the later gospels.

We did not attempt to carry this trajectory back to the ministry of Jesus. It is not unlikely that Jesus asked his followers to expand his work through missions of their own, and the mission instructions reflect the radical edge of his message of the kingdom. Nevertheless, it is impossible to recover what Jesus' actual words might have been, for the mission instructions bear too clearly the imprint of those who later preserved them. Thus we began with a mission movement in rural Palestine in the first decades after Easter.

If our reconstruction has been correct, at an early stage the mission instructions shaped and were shaped by a movement characterized by radical poverty and radical itinerancy. Not all of early Christianity shared this ethos, not even all of early Palestinian Christianity. The bearers of this tradition were a special group called to a special life-style and with a special message. In many ways these traveling missionaries would have resembled the Cynics. Both groups traveled light, minced no words, and, as for the *ideal* Cynics and mission workers at least, accepted provisions only from those who had heard and received their message. The mission instructions were not formulated, however, with this comparison in mind. They were primarily shaped by theological concerns.

The significance for this movement of asking for money or support is rather ambiguous. In part this is due to the indirect nature of the evidence: We had to reconstruct the early form of the mission instructions from conflicting versions in the gospels. Yet there also seems to be an inherent ambiguity in the act of asking for money. If the mission workers viewed an offer of hospitality as a sign of receptivity to their message of the kingdom, a request for hospitality—food and lodging—could serve as a test for this receptivity. On the other hand, requests for money and support seem to contradict the basic ethos of the movement—radical trust in God.

At any rate, explicit comments on *asking* for money do not seem to have been a part of the early instructions. Later, however, there were some striking changes. In part these were due to the shift in perspective from that of the mission workers to that of the host communities. In part, though, they were due to the rise of corruption in the ranks of the mission workers. This corruption of the movement clarified the question of asking for money. Matthew and the *Didache*, for example, show no ambivalence: Asking for money for personal needs was not permitted. It became a sign of the false prophet. Luke, on the other hand, does not explicitly reject the practice of asking for money nor does he explicitly condone it. He is clearly aware that changing circumstances, especially increased hostility, have had an effect on the mission movement, and he makes it clear that mission workers deserve their wages. This may presuppose an approval of the practice of asking for money, but the question is not directly addressed.

The gospels thus do not leave us with a firm starting point in our quest for New Testament perspectives on the activity of asking for money. The earliest position we can recover is a radical trust that was essentially unconcerned about questions of monetary support. With the appearance of corruption in the movement, mission workers were explicitly prohibited from asking for money and hospitality was inculcated in the churches to meet the needs of the workers. Luke shows an awareness that the new context of the mission required new arrangements for the mission workers, but he provides no reflections on the appropriate methods of soliciting funds. For that we need to turn to Paul.

FOR FURTHER READING

Analysis and evaluation of the gospel material is complicated by the fact that the first three gospels are connected by a complex literary relationship. At various points in this chapter, I have indicated the probable nature of this relationship, but I did not formally discuss the "Two Source

Hypothesis" that defines it nor did I mention alternative hypotheses that have been proposed. To do so would have meant a lengthy technical discussion unsuited to the goals of this book. Interested readers, however, are encouraged to consult the articles entitled "The Synoptic Problem" in Volume 4 and the Supplementary Volume of *The Interpreter's Dictionary of the Bible* (Nashville: Abingdon, 1962 and 1976), though any introduction to the New Testament will address this question. For a good overview of the presumed written source in which Matthew and Luke found the more rigorous form of the mission instructions, see Ivan Havener's book *Q: The Sayings of Jesus* (Wilmington, Del.: Michael Glazier, 1987). ("Q," short for the German word *Quelle* or source, is the name scholars have given to this hypothetical document.) A particularly good discussion of the factors that shaped the stories about Jesus during the period of their oral transmission can be found in the chapter "Jesus in the Memory of the Church" in Luke T. Johnson's *Writings of the New Testament: An Interpretation* (Philadelphia: Fortress Press, 1986).

I have followed the convention of referring to the first three evangelists as "Matthew," "Mark," and "Luke," but the question of the authorship of the gospels is far more complex than these familiar names would indicate. In chapter 4 ("Problems of Introduction–II") of his book *Reading the New Testament: Methods of Interpretation* (Philadelphia: Fortress Press, 1987), Christopher Tuckett gives a balanced discussion of the issues involved in assessing the authorship of the New Testament writings. In fact, the entire book is highly recommended as an introduction to and assessment of the various ways scholars examine the New Testament. For specific discussions of the authorship of the first three gospels, the reader should consult the entries on these gospels in *The Interpreter's Dictionary of the Bible* or in *Harper's Bible Commentary* (San Francisco: Harper & Row, Publishers, 1988).

Martin Hengel's book *Property and Riches in the Early Church*

(Philadelphia: Fortress Press, 1974) gives a nice but rather brief overview of attitudes toward money in the early church. More focused and considerably more sophisticated are the works of Gerd Theissen, who has explored the social world of early Palestinian Christianity. Theissen has identified wandering charismatics as a significant feature of that social world and has attempted to define not only the characteristics of that movement but also the sociological factors that contributed to its emergence. I have relied on a number of his insights though I have quoted his work only a few times. The quotation on page 41 above is taken from "Itinerant Radicalism: The Tradition of Jesus' Sayings from the Perspective of the Sociology of Literature," *Radical Religion* 2, nos. 2-3 (1975), pages 84-93, which contains his most thorough analysis of the mission instructions. The definition of "charismatic" (page 43 above) is quoted from page 8 of his book *Sociology of Early Palestinian Christianity* (Philadelphia: Fortress Press, 1978), and the thesis of charismatic begging (page 43 above) is quoted from an essay entitled "Legitimation and Subsistence" found in *The Social Setting of Pauline Christianity: Essays on Corinth,* ed. John H. Schutz (Philadelphia: Fortress Press, 1982), page 31.

Theissen's work has been very influential among New Testament scholars, though it is not without critics. Wolfgang Stegemann, for example, challenges Theissen's thesis of a life-style of voluntary renunciation in his essay "Vagabond Radicalism in Early Christianity?" found in *God of the Lowly: Socio-Historical Interpretations of the Bible,* ed. W. Schottroff and W. Stegemann (Maryknoll, N.Y.: Orbis Books, 1984), but his argument has an ideological bias that renders it unconvincing. A more serious criticism is that Theissen, while recognizing the social complexity of the period, has failed to do justice to the literary complexity of the gospels. Risto Uro's impressive work on the mission instructions, *Sheep Among the Wolves: A Study of the Mission Instructions of Q* (Helsinki: Suomalainen Tiedeakatemia,

1987), while narrower in scope than Theissen's, employs greater methodological rigor in dealing with the texts. I have followed his reconstruction of the early rigorous version of these instructions. Ferdinand Hahn devotes a few pages to an analysis of Jesus' words of commission in his book *Mission in the New Testament* (Studies in Biblical Theology 47; London: SCM Press, 1965), pages 41-46, but his focus is on the question of the authenticity of these words, not on the nature of the movement that preserved them after Jesus' death.

The commentaries are very uneven in their treatment of these instructions. Francis W. Beare's commentary *The Gospel According to Matthew* (San Francisco: Harper & Row, Publishers, 1981) provides a good discussion, though his article "The Mission of the Disciples and the Mission Charge: Matthew 10 and Parallels," *The Journal of Biblical Literature* 89 (1970), pages 1-13, is more thorough. Robert A. Guelich offers a sensitive analysis of Mark's mission instructions in *Mark 1–8:26* (Word Biblical Commentary 34A; Dallas, Tex.: Word, 1989), and Joseph A. Fitzmyer's two-volume Anchor Bible Commentary (Garden City, N.Y.: Doubleday, 1981 and 1985) presents the best analysis of Luke's treatment of the instructions.

I have quoted the *Didache* from Kirsopp Lake's translation in the Loeb Classical Library, *Apostolic Fathers*, vol. 1 (Cambridge, Mass.: Harvard University Press, 1912).

CHAPTER 3

PERSPECTIVES FROM PAUL, 1:
MONEY AND MISSION

From Jerusalem and as far around as Illyricum
I have fully proclaimed the good news of Christ.
—*Romans 15:19*

These words that Paul wrote to the church at Rome may have contained some rhetorical exaggeration, for as far as we know Paul had not actually preached in Jerusalem and had done no missionary work inside Illyricum (present-day Yugoslavia). Nevertheless, even a casual glance at a map of Paul's journeys reveals that the distances he traveled were very impressive. Paul covered, by one estimate, more than 10,000 miles as he criss-crossed by land and by sea the northeast quadrant of the Mediterranean basin. The letters confirm the impression of almost constant travel, and not just by Paul himself. After leaving a church he stayed in close touch with it by sending coworkers back to visit: Timothy, for example, to Thessalonica (I Thess. 3:2), to Corinth (I Cor. 4:17), and to Philippi (Phil. 2:19-24), and Titus to Corinth (II Cor 7:6-16; 8:6). Paul also refers to plans for travel by even larger delegations (I Cor. 16:3-4; II Cor. 8:16-24) as well as to his own elaborate plans for future journeys to Jerusalem, Rome, and Spain (Rom. 15:23-29). All of this travel required money, money for passage on ships, money for land transportation, and, of course, money for food and for inns. To be sure, whenever he could Paul made use of the hospitality of Christian homes during his travels (Philem. 22; Rom. 16:23), but often this was not possible since he was constantly pushing the frontier of the Christian mission into new "unchurched" regions, "not where Christ has already been named, so that I do not build on someone else's foundation" (Rom. 15:20).

There were other expenses as well: living expenses when he stayed in a city for what were sometimes extended periods of time, and the expenses required to maintain the network of coworkers that held the fragile Pauline mission field together. Some expenses we can only guess at. Did the secretaries who wrote Paul's letters (Rom. 16:22; *see also* I Cor. 16:21; Gal. 6:11) volunteer their labors? Were those who carried the letters to and from Paul reimbursed for this time-consuming work? Paul's expenses may have been modest by our standards, but compared with the financial requirements of the original mission in Palestine, his missionary activity was expensive indeed. It is thus not surprising that Paul's letters contain numerous references to the question of remuneration. What *is* perhaps surprising is the complexity of the answers that Paul supplies.

Perhaps the most obvious and striking aspect of Paul's comments on remuneration, especially in the light of the numerous expenses connected with his missionary work, is his emphatic refusal to ask for or accept recompense for this work (I Thess. 2:9; I Cor. 9:11-18; II Cor. 2:17; 11:7-11; 12:14). We need to look very carefully at this "policy," if indeed it is such. First we need to look at the reasons Paul presents for adhering to this policy, since the theological or ethical grounds for *not* asking for money are surely as relevant to our quest as any grounds he may present *for* asking for funds. Second, we need to look carefully at this policy because, emphatic as he seems about it, Paul did not always follow it. When did Paul break with this policy and why? What do these exceptions say about Paul's understanding of the wider implications of asking for money? Finally, we need to look carefully at this policy because it seems to have gotten Paul into a lot of trouble with at least one of his churches. How did these problems arise and what can we learn from Paul's mistakes, if such they be?

There is one other source we can use for information

about Paul's thoughts on asking for money: his letter to Philemon, to which we will turn at the end of the chapter. Paul does not directly ask for money in this short letter, but he does ask for an expensive favor, and the way he frames and supports this request should be relevant to our question.

A FISCAL POLICY: I CORINTHIANS

Three times in the ninth chapter of I Corinthians Paul emphasizes his refusal to accept money in return for his preaching: "What then is my reward? Just this: that in my proclamation I may make the gospel free of charge, so as not to make full use of my rights in the gospel" (I Cor. 9:18; *see also* vv. 12, 15). Such emphasis is striking and surely significant, yet it is not immediately clear why Paul introduces this subject here. In chapter 8 he has addressed the question of whether Christians could eat food that had been offered to idols, and in chapter 10 he continues his discussion of that subject. In chapter 9, however, Paul interrupts this discussion of eating taboos with what seems to be a spirited defense of his apostleship: "Am I not free? Am I not an apostle? Have I not seen Jesus our Lord? Are you not my work in the Lord?" (9:1). The shift in tone as well as content strikes some scholars as so dramatic that they take it as evidence that chapter 9 is a later insertion or that it acquired its current peculiar location in the letter through some accidental rearrangement of Paul's original argument. Others, however, insist that its placement is not only deliberate but also rhetorically sound.

In chapters 8 and 10 Paul argues that Christians are free to eat whatever they like: "'Food will not bring us close to God.' We are no worse off if we do not eat, and no better off if we do" (8:8; *see also* 10:25-27). Yet Paul then calls upon the Corinthians to relinquish their Christian freedom if and when another Christian is offended by it (8:9-13; 10:28-33). Though different in content, chapter 9 seems admirably crafted to support this argument, for in it Paul not only defends his right to apostolic privileges but also renounces these same privileges when doing so advances the cause of the gospel. Paul thus presents himself as an example of the behavior he is asking of the Corinthians (*see* 11:1). Yet if the primary purpose of the chapter is to provide an example of appropriate behavior, why is Paul's "defense" so spirited? Was he also responding in this chapter to actual accusations of inappropriate apostolic behavior or even a lack of apostolic status? Some insist that this must be so, especially since these same accusations are clearly present, as we will see, at the time Paul wrote II Corinthians. In I Corinthians, however, Paul does not seem to view the situation as critical, for his response to his personal detractors (if there were such) is subordinated to his concern to instruct the Corinthian church in the correct use of Christian freedom. We cannot expect, then, a straightforward discussion of the question of remuneration, for Paul has another issue— Christian freedom—in mind. Yet we need to look at the reasons Paul gives in this context for refusing to ask for monetary support.

First he insists on his right to support, using words that echo the Lukan mission instructions: "Do we not have the right to our food and drink? Do we not have the right to be accompanied by a believing wife, as do the other apostles and the brothers of the Lord and Cephas? Or is it only Barnabas and I who have no right to refrain from working for a living?" (9:4-6). It is clear from his argument here that other apostles do accept support, and Paul does not criticize them for this. As apostles they—and Paul—have an undeniable right to support from their churches, because the churches have received such undeniable benefits from their work: "If we have sown spiritual good among you, is it too much if we reap your material benefits? If others share this rightful claim on you, do not we still more?" (vv. 11-12*a*). Yet Paul insists that he does not—and will not—make use of this right. He mentions this now to encourage the Corinthians to similar acts of self-denial, but what were his original reasons for refusing support?

The first time Paul raises this point his explanation is brief: "Nevertheless, we have not made use of this right [to monetary recompense], but we endure anything rather than put an obstacle in the way of the gospel of Christ" (v. 12*b*). Several things are clear from this statement. First—and emphatically—this is a voluntary action, a voluntary renunciation of what is otherwise an incontestable right. Second, when Paul speaks of "enduring anything" he seems to suggest that the renunciation could involve a real sacrifice. At the very least it would seem to involve enduring working at a secular job to cover expenses while at the same time proclaiming the gospel (I Cor. 4:11-12*a*; I Thess. 2:9). The reason Paul supplies for making this sacrifice is to avoid placing an *obstacle* in the way of the gospel. What sort of obstacle does Paul have in mind? Various suggestions have been made. Paul may have feared that asking for or accepting money would generate the appearance of greed (I Thess. 2:5); that it would evoke an inappropriate image of the missionary as a peddler of God's word (II Cor. 2:17); or that it would impose an intolerable financial burden on the struggling young congregations (I Thess. 2:9; II Cor. 11:9). Paul's concern here may simply have been a legacy of his Pharisaic past, though it was only later that the rabbis articulated as a firm principle the idea that no payment was to be accepted for teaching the Law. In this chapter, however, Paul does not mention any of these concrete possibilities.

Since the argument of chapters 8–10 is, in spite of appearances to the contrary, a unity, the obstacle Paul mentions here is probably related to the stumbling block he refers to in 8:9: "But take care that this liberty of yours [regarding eating meat] does not *somehow* become a stumbling block to the weak." Paul makes a similar comment in chapter 10: "Give *no* offense to Jews or to Greeks or to the church of God" (v. 32). It is not necessary, then, to isolate the specific obstacle, for the general admonition in all these chapters is to endure *all* things lest *any* obstacle be placed in the way of the gospel. Paul's only point, then, is the primacy of the gospel. If requesting remuneration puts any sort of obstacle in the way of his proclamation of the gospel—and Paul is obviously convinced that with this church at this time it does—then he will not ask for his rightful recompense.

Paul's basic point here is the issue of priorities, not principles. He is not *on principle* opposed to remuneration. Indeed, as an apostle he has acquired the right to receive material support from his congregations. But as an apostle he has also been charged with the task of preaching the gospel, and when his right to support endangers the successful completion of his charge, the charge to preach the gospel must prevail.

After making this point, Paul begins citing more support in favor of his right to remuneration (9:13-14), only to insist once again that he has not made use of this right and does not intend to make use of it. This time his explanation is more impassioned and grounded more psychologically than pragmatically. It is also somewhat less clear:

> But I have made no use of any of these rights, nor am I writing this so that they may be applied in my case. Indeed, I would rather die than that—no one will deprive me of my ground for boasting! If I proclaim the gospel, this gives me no ground for boasting, for an obligation is laid on me, and woe to me if I do not proclaim the gospel! For if I do this of my own will, I have a reward; but if not of my own will, I am entrusted with a commission. What then is my reward? Just this: that in my proclamation I may make the gospel free of charge, so as not to make full use of my rights in the gospel.
> (9:15-18)

The problem is that Paul's argument shifts rather abruptly here. He first claims to have a ground for boasting but denies that proclaiming the gospel provides this ground, for this proclaiming was done under compulsion. But instead of continuing by giving the ground he *does* have for boasting, he shifts his argument to talk of reward. We can guess from the direction the argument was moving that the ground for boasting that Paul had in mind was his commitment to proclaiming the gospel *without cost to the community,* for in that policy Paul goes beyond his commission, beyond even what the other apostles were doing. But he does not explicitly say this. Perhaps he changed his line of argument here because his usual position on boasting was to exclude it as a theologically illegitimate attitude, unless it was boasting in God or in the human weakness that reveals the power of the cross (I Cor. 1:31; II Cor. 11:30). For whatever reason, though, Paul shifts from talk of boasting to talk of reward and engages in a little play on words. Since he is under compulsion to proclaim the gospel, he has no right to expect a reward (literally a "wage"). Yet in fact he does receive a reward or wage. His very refusal to accept a wage *is* his wage, for the gospel is the center of his life, and acting in a way that facilitates its spread is a source of great personal, if not material, satisfaction. If the humor here is too convoluted for our taste, Paul's commitment to the gospel is clear: "Woe to me if I do not proclaim the gospel!"

The tone of these verses suggests, as we noted above, that some sort of accusation lies behind them. Perhaps it is rooted in the contrast between Paul's policy and that of the other apostles, but it does not explicitly surface in Paul's argument. Instead he retreats from the emotional tone of these verses and goes on to show that his policy with regard to remuneration is part of his larger missionary strategy of becoming a "slave to all, so that I might win more of them" (I Cor. 9:19). He concludes this portion of his argument by emphasizing once again his basic commitment: "I do all things *for the sake of the gospel*" (v. 23, my translation).

CONFLICT OVER THE POLICY: II CORINTHIANS

The question of material support for apostolic labors becomes even more acute in Paul's later correspondence with the Corinthian church, where the same issue is addressed but with a new sense of urgency and conflict:

> Did I commit a sin by humbling myself so that you might be exalted, because I proclaimed God's good news to you free of charge? I robbed other churches by accepting support from them in order to serve you. And when I was with you and was in need, I did not burden anyone, for my needs were supplied by the friends who came from Macedonia. So I refrained and will continue to refrain from burdening you in any way. As the truth of Christ is in me, this boast of mine will not be silenced in the regions of Achaia. And why? Because I do not love you? God knows I do! (II Cor. 11:7-11)

Paul's stance here is the same, but the change in mood is rather striking. In I Corinthians 9 Paul spoke of the *reward* he derives from not accepting money, hinting at his almost illegitimate pride at being able to present the gospel free of charge. In *this* letter Paul refers to his policy in terms of *humbling* himself, of "committing a sin." These words are ironic, of course, but they suggest, as do the repeated oaths ("As the truth of Christ is in me!" "God knows I do!"), that Paul is responding to some rather pointed accusations. Clearly something has happened in this church. The murmurings of discontent that Paul essentially ignored in I Corinthians 9 have here erupted into open conflict that he is forced to confront. What caused this turn of events?

The issue here is what Bengt Holmberg refers to as the connection (always complex) between money relations and authority relations, a connection that was highlighted by the appearance in Corinth of rivals to Paul's leadership. New apostles had arrived with a different message (II Cor. 11:4) and a different attitude toward recompense (11:20). They suggested that Paul was an inadequate apostle (10:10; 11:5-6), and his refusal to accept money for his apostolic labors contributed substantially to this impression (12:11-13). The Corinthians were persuaded by this argument, for in contrast to these "super-apostles" (11:5; 12:11) Paul did seem somewhat inferior. Indeed, as E. A. Judge has suggested, the Corinthians probably began to feel embarrassed for Paul, especially if he supported himself by manual labor while in their midst (I Cor. 4:11-12a). It is, however, not just a question of Paul's authority. The community's sense of its own status seems to have been threatened by Paul's actions. Whatever his motives, by refusing to take money from them Paul has refused to recognize them as legitimate benefactors, and this suggests, or so the "super-apostles" have implied, that Paul does not esteem them very highly (II Cor. 11:11).

In this context Paul was forced to defend—or abandon—his actions, and characteristically he chose the former. Paul's angry and hurt response appears most clearly in the words quoted above, in which he protests his love and defends his motives, but earlier in this letter he made some other comments that seem, in retrospect, to be relevant to this dispute. In II Corinthians 6:3-10 there is no explicit reference to financial issues, but there seem to be allusions to them throughout the passage:

> We are putting no obstacle in anyone's way, so that no fault may be found with our ministry, but as servants of God we have commended ourselves in every way: through great endurance, in afflictions, hardships, calamities, beatings, imprisonments, riots, labors, sleepless nights, hunger; by purity, knowledge, patience, kindness, holiness of spirit, genuine love, truthful speech, and the power of God; with the weapons of righteousness for the right hand and for the left; in honor and dishonor, in ill repute and good repute. We are treated as impostors, and yet are true; as unknown, and yet are well known; as dying, and see—we are alive; as punished, and yet not killed; as sorrowful, yet always rejoicing; as poor, yet making many rich; as having nothing, and yet possessing everything.

Here Paul refers again to his concern over creating obstacles to the promulgation of the gospel, but in this text it is clear that Paul now has a very particular obstacle in mind: the challenge to the integrity of his ministry. As in I Corinthians 9, Paul says that rather than create obstacles, he will endure whatever is necessary, and that includes not only afflictions and hardships but "labors" as well. Paul does not describe what he means by "labors," but the same word is used in I Corinthians 4:12 and I Thessalonians 2:9, where he describes the work with which he financed his apostolic mission. Other phrases in this passage suggest that the conflict over finances is not far from Paul's thoughts: "We are treated as impostors," "as poor, yet making many rich," "as having nothing, and yet possessing everything." What is particularly interesting about this passage, though, is that Paul maintains that his endurance in the face of these hardships, financial and otherwise, commend him as a servant of God. Here Paul is beginning to develop a more explicitly *theological* warrant for his actions. He endures all things, including the burden of supporting his own ministry, not only for the sake of the gospel, not only for the sake of his own personal satisfaction, but also because by doing so he demonstrates what it means to be God's "servants" (literally, *diakonoi*). We see more evidence of the argument in 11:7-11, quoted above.

As we saw, in II Corinthians 11:7-11 Paul directly confronts accusations concerning his financial arrangements. He also makes explicit what earlier he was hesitant to say: that preaching the gospel free of charge provides him grounds for boasting. The verses that follow this passage develop this point, though in a somewhat convoluted fashion: "And what I do I will also continue to do, in order to deny an opportunity to those who want an opportunity to be recognized as our equals in what they boast about. For such boasters are false apostles, deceitful workers, disguising themselves as apostles of Christ" (vv. 12-13). Paul's actions concerning finances are intended, he now says, to expose the newcomers in Corinth as "false apostles, deceitful workers."

Throughout this letter Paul has made it clear that the

sacrifices he makes on behalf of his churches—which would seem to include supporting himself financially—are not incidental to his ministry but reflect its essential message. Already in I Corinthians, Paul insisted that the cross demands a reevaluation of the world and its wisdom (I Cor. 1:18-31). He repeats that message with even greater emphasis in his later correspondence with this church. Paul's weaknesses and sufferings—and *only* his weaknesses and sufferings—provide him with grounds for boasting, for just as God's power was revealed in the absurdity of the cross, so it continues to be revealed through the fragility of the vessels that God uses to proclaim the gospel (II Cor. 4:7-12). Quite explicitly, it seems, Paul includes his labors on behalf of the church as an example of the "weakness" that aligns him with the cross:

> . . . in toil and hardship, through many a sleepless night, hungry and thirsty, often without food, cold and naked. And, besides other things, I am under daily pressure because of my anxiety for all the churches. Who is weak, and I am not weak? Who is made to stumble, and I am not indignant? If I must boast, I will boast of the things that show my weakness.
> (II Cor. 11:27-30)

Thus Paul insists that his life-style—including the hardships engendered by his unorthodox manner of financing his work—is an extension of his message. Paul, then, does not simply *sever* the connection between financial relations and authority relations, but using the cross as his warrant, he *inverts* the connection. The wisdom of the age suggests that asking for financial support implies the possession of full apostolic authority. Paul counters with the claim that by renouncing this support he embraces a life-style that renders him an even better servant of Christ and of God.

Paul's argument concerning finances has changed considerably in the course of his dispute with the Corinthian church. Requesting and not requesting financial support are no longer presented as equally valid options for apostles of Christ, to be chosen on pragmatic grounds. The issue is now couched in terms of true versus false apostles, and the very truth of the Christian message is at stake. In these circumstances there is only *one* option for the true apostle of Christ. The significance of asking for money is thus not static. The message conveyed by acceptance or nonacceptance of funds changes with the circumstances, and when these circumstances threaten the truth of the Christian message, a pragmatic option hardens into a restrictive principle: "For we cannot do anything against the truth, but only for the truth" (II Cor. 13:8).

At least one other significant point is emphasized in this passage: Paul's concern not to "burden" the church: "And when I was with you and was in need, I did not *burden* anyone, for my needs were supplied by the friends who came from Macedonia. So I refrained and will continue to refrain from *burdening* you in any way" (11:9, emphasis added). Paul picks up this idea of burdening again in the next chapter and develops it with such fierce irony that it must somehow define a point of real controversy between himself and the false apostles:

> How have you been worse off than the other churches, except that I myself did not *burden* you? Forgive me this wrong! Here I am, ready to come to you this third time. And I will not be a *burden,* because I do not want what is yours but you; for children ought not to lay up for their parents, but parents for their children. (12:13-14)

Even in a context that shows less strain of controversy and personal attack, Paul expresses his concern not to be a burden to the churches to which he ministers (I Thess. 2:9). Thus alongside Paul's concern for the gospel as a determining factor in his financial arrangements with his churches, there emerges a concern for the churches, their circumstances, and their resources. Paul, though willing himself to endure anything for the sake of the gospel, is not willing—in certain circumstances at least—to place an undue financial burden on his churches. Yet, as we will see, the concept of "burden" is quite subjective, and some impoverished Pauline churches saw the opportunity to give as a source of joy rather than resentment.

ANOTHER FISCAL POLICY: PHILIPPIANS

Paul's financial relationship with the church in Corinth was thus surprisingly complex and tense, and it clearly deteriorated over time. We have seen that one reason for this was the arrival in Corinth of rival leaders. Another possible reason, however, emerges in Paul's heated response, for even while defending his refusal to accept money from the Corinthians, Paul acknowledges that for some time he has been accepting it from other churches: "I robbed other churches by accepting support from them in order to serve you . . . for my needs were supplied by the friends who came from Macedonia" (II Cor. 11:8-9). Paul, it seems, was not absolutely consistent in his financial arrangements, and his celebrated apostolic flexibility ("I have become all things to all people, that I might by all means save some," I Cor. 9:22), when applied to matters of money, probably exacerbated the friction with this church.

Consider the picture that is emerging. In I Corinthians Paul protested that he made no use of his apostolic right to financial support (9:12, 15, 18), suggesting that instead he supported himself by his own labors (4:12). In II Corinthians, however, he reveals that at the same time that he was proclaiming the gospel without cost to the Corinthians he was accepting support from other churches, and mentions explicitly support from Macedonia. The city of Philippi is in Macedonia, and Paul's letter to the church in this city reveals that they were indeed regular supporters of his ministry (Phil. 4:15-16). He also mentions in that letter that they

75

supported him while he was in Thessalonica, yet in Paul's correspondence with the Thessalonians he again makes no mention of this support, relating instead that he "worked night and day, so that we might not burden any of you while we proclaimed to you the gospel of God" (I Thess. 2:9). Small wonder then that the Corinthians accused him of vacillation (II Cor. 1:17) and even of guile (12:16).

Now it is possible to harmonize these comments. If one assumes, for example, that the support mentioned in II Corinthians 11 began *after* Paul had written I Corinthians 9, and Philippians 4:10 does hint at a delay, then Paul's comments are not incompatible. Such harmonizations, however, are not really necessary. None of these passages is anything like a financial disclosure statement. Each one is part of a larger argument or defense that determines what Paul emphasizes about his actions. Paul may simply have focused too much on the immediate argument and not enough on the whole picture, little suspecting the problems this would later create. The question is whether we can learn anything from Paul's flexible arrangements. What justification does he provide for his willingness to accept funds from one church even while rejecting them from another? We need to look carefully at his words to the Philippians:

> It is a great joy to me, in the Lord, that after so long your care for me has now blossomed afresh. You did care about me before for that matter; it was opportunity that you lacked. Not that I am alluding to want, for I have learned to find resources in myself whatever my circumstances. I know what it is to be brought low, and I know what it is to have plenty. I have been very thoroughly initiated into the human lot with all its ups and downs—fullness and hunger, plenty and want. I have strength for anything through him who gives me power. But it was kind of you to share the burden of my troubles.
>
> As you know yourselves, Philippians, in the early days of my mission, when I set out from Macedonia, you alone of all our congregations were my partners in payments and receipts; for even at Thessalonica you contributed to my

needs, not once but twice over. Do not think I set my heart upon the gift; all I care for is the profit accruing to you. However, here I give you my receipt for everything—for more than everything; I am paid in full, now that I have received from Epaphroditus what you sent. It is a fragrant offering, an acceptable sacrifice, pleasing to God. And my God will supply all your wants out of the magnificence of his riches in Christ Jesus. To our God and Father be glory for endless ages! Amen. (Phil. 4:10-20)

I have quoted this rather extensive passage from the New English Bible, for it brings out a bit more clearly than the New Revised Standard Version a peculiar quality of Paul's language here: his frequent use, especially in the second paragraph, of terms from the business world. Note the phrases "partners in payments and receipts," "profit accruing to you," "I give you my receipt," and "paid in full." Though some commentators dismiss this language as "playful" or as a sign of Paul's embarrassment, it defines an important aspect of the relationship between Paul and this particular church. In fact, Paul seems to view the Philippians' recent gift as part of a formal partnership *(koinonia)* they have entered into with Paul for the spread of the gospel.

Paul often mentions *koinonia,* more than any other New Testament writer, and the word takes on a range of meanings. He speaks of the Christians' fellowship *(koinonia)* with Christ (I Cor. 1:9) and with the Holy Spirit (II Cor. 13:14; Phil. 2:1), he describes their participation *(koinonia)* in the body and blood of Christ through the Lord's Supper (I Cor. 10:16), and he also speaks, especially in Philippians, of their partnership *(koinonia)* with the gospel and with him.

Paul mentions this partnership in the gospel early in the letter (Phil. 1:5) and then picks up the idea later with the reference in 4:15 to a "partnership with me in giving and receiving" (RSV). This phrase seems to suggest more than the Philippians giving and Paul receiving. In the wider context of the letter, it seems clear that Paul views the Philippians' gift as part of a much larger pattern of reciprocity that embraces Paul, the Philippians, the gospel, and God. The Philippians have received the word of grace, and in return they have volunteered, or been asked, to sponsor Paul's continuing apostolic work, that is, to become Paul's "partner." This giving, Paul says, will in turn redound to their own credit (4:17), and they will once again become beneficiaries of God's largess (v. 19). In fact, in verse 18 Paul uses sacrificial language to suggest that their gift to him is really a gift to God, "a fragrant offering, a sacrifice acceptable and pleasing to God" (NRSV), and one to which God will respond. This expected response thus closes the circle of benefaction.

It is important to note the significance of the "partnership" language in this argument. Not only are the Philippians sharers *(koinoi)* with Paul in grace (1:7) and in affliction (4:14), common participants in the body of Christ, they are also linked with Paul by a special relationship. Sometimes Paul needed to assert his authority in that relationship and he did so by referring to his apostolic status or by describing himself as the "father" of the church. But when this relationship was healthy and mature, as it was with the Philippians, Paul could speak of a *partnership* with the church in the gospel. Indeed, Holmberg argues that the presence of this relationship of mutual trust and understanding is a necessary criterion for Paul to accept money from that church, and perhaps to ask for it as well. When this relationship is present, financial support becomes a natural expression not only of the church's solidarity with Paul but also of its understanding of the reciprocity of the Christian life. Those who have received will also give, and categories of spiritual and material benefits become interchangeable. When this relationship is *not* present, however, money is instead a potential offense, a stumbling block and a burden to the church.

The importance and seriousness of this partnership relationship, then, is emphasized by the business terminology that Paul uses in this passage in Philippians. In one verse in this letter, Paul even describes their gift as, literally, "supplying the shortfall in your service to me" (2:30, my translation). The word for "service" (*leitourgia*) is the technical term often used to describe the nearly obligatory "donations" that were part of the system of benefaction in the Roman world. Thus Paul seems to *expect* the partnership to result in financial support, yet he also seems concerned to avoid *misuse* of the partnership. Many have noted his curious tentativeness in this passage. Though clearly appreciative of the money the Philippians have sent, Paul does not ever *directly* express his gratitude to them. But according to the rather rigid patterns of reciprocity that structured the concept of benefaction, to do so would have placed the Philippians under new obligation to send more, and Paul clearly does not want to do that. Thus he uses business terminology to temper and control his gratitude and to indicate that the debt has been fully discharged: "I give you my receipt for everything . . . I am paid in full" (4:18, NEB). He also shifts to sacrificial terminology to deflect the gift—and the benefactor relationship—from himself to God. Paul's letter to the Philippians thus suggests that *koinonia*, a sense of partnership with Paul and participation in the gospel, are critical factors in Paul's financial arrangements with a church.

Yet we must be careful not to overinterpret Paul's words here. When Paul speaks of the Philippians' financial support, he rather clearly indicates *when* that support began: "when I *left* Macedonia" (4:15). Thus we have no evidence that the Philippians, any more than the Corinthians, supported Paul while he was working among them, but only as he left to carry the gospel to other locations. The timing of their gift suggests that it was intended to promote the sending forth of the gospel, and this was so common a practice that the word used to describe it, *propempein,* became a technical term in the Pauline mission field. This word literally means "to accompany," but in the mission field it came to have a more specific meaning: to equip someone for the continuation of a journey by providing food, money, guides, traveling company, and by making any necessary arrangements for passage on a ship. The usual translation in the New Revised Standard Version (to be sent on one's way) masks somewhat the financial obligations inherent in this activity.

In Romans 15:24 we see that Paul expects this support from the Roman church, which he has never met. Even more striking, however, is the fact that Paul expects the same sort of financial send-off from the Corinthians, from whom he has proudly refused to accept remuneration for his work among them (I Cor. 16:6). Not only that, he expects the same support for his associates when they pass through (I Cor. 16:11). When viewed against this background, the Philippians' support seems to be just another instance of this financial sending forth, yet the arrangement with the Philippians did have a few distinctive elements. Paul indicates not only that the Philippians were the only ones in Macedonia actually to provide the financial assistance required to move the gospel to a new region, but also that they continued to do this after he had left. It is this continuing support that seems to have been rooted in the special *koinonia* that church shared with Paul.

Our discussion so far has been teased out of indirect evidence. Clearly financial matters are a constant concern to Paul and to his churches, but we have not yet seen him explicitly asking for support for his apostolic labors. In several letters he makes a point of *not* asking for money, while in Philippians we enter the conversation too late: He is rendering thanks for a gift already received. To hear Paul's explicit warrants for remuneration we have to turn to Philemon. In this short letter Paul is still not asking for monetary support, but he *is* asking for an expensive personal favor, the release to him of a slave. We need to look at how he couches and supports this request.

A DELICATE REQUEST: PHILEMON

Paul's letter to Philemon is distinctive in the Pauline corpus. Short and personal, it is the only one of the undisputed letters that is addressed to an individual. (I and II Timothy and Titus are also addressed to individuals, but many scholars are convinced that these letters, though presented in Paul's name, were not actually written by him.) It is possible, and probably worthwhile, to quote the entire letter:

Paul, a prisoner of Christ Jesus, and Timothy our brother, To Philemon our dear friend and co-worker, to Apphia our sister, to Archippus our fellow soldier, and to the church in your house:

Grace to you and peace from God our Father and the Lord Jesus Christ.

When I remember you in my prayers, I always thank my God because I hear of your love for all the saints and your faith toward the Lord Jesus. I pray that the sharing of your faith may become effective when you perceive all the good that we may do for Christ. I have indeed received much joy and encouragement from your love, because the hearts of the saints have been refreshed through you, my brother.

For this reason, though I am bold enough in Christ to command you to do your duty, yet I would rather appeal to you on the basis of love—and I, Paul, do this as an old man, and now also as a prisoner of Christ Jesus. I am appealing to you for my child, Onesimus, whose father I have become during my imprisonment. Formerly he was useless to you, but now he is indeed useful both to you and to me. I am sending him, that is, my own heart, back to you. I wanted to keep him with me, so that he might be of service to me in your place during my imprisonment for the gospel; but I preferred to do nothing without your consent, in order that your good deed might be voluntary and not something forced. Perhaps this is the reason he was separated from you for a while, so that you might have him back forever, no longer as a slave but more than a slave, a beloved brother—especially to me but how much more to you, both in the flesh and in the Lord.

So if you consider me your partner, welcome him as you would welcome me. If he has wronged you in any way, or owes you anything, charge that to my account. I, Paul, am writing this with my own hand: I will repay it. I say nothing about your owing me even your own self. Yes, brother, let me have this benefit from you in the Lord! Refresh my heart in Christ. Confident of your obedience, I am writing to you, knowing that you will do even more than I say.

One thing more—prepare a guest room for me, for I am hoping through your prayers to be restored to you.

Epaphras, my fellow prisoner in Christ Jesus, sends greetings to you, and so do Mark, Aristarchus, Demas, and Luke, my fellow workers.

The grace of the Lord Jesus Christ be with your spirit.

The situation that Paul is addressing can easily be reconstructed from this letter. Onesimus, a slave, has run away from his master Philemon and has somehow ended up with Paul, ministering to the apostle while he is in prison. He has also been converted by Paul, and now Paul is sending him back to his master, who is also one of Paul's converts. Indeed, Paul is compelled by Roman law to return the fugitive, but with the slave he sends this letter requesting not only that Philemon accept him back without reprisal, even for the items Onesimus may have stolen (v. 18), but that he accept him back "no longer as a slave but . . . a beloved brother" (v. 16). Indeed, many scholars are convinced that when Paul closes the letter with the words, "Confident of your obedience, I am writing to you, knowing that you will do *even more than I say*" (v. 21, emphasis added), Paul is actually asking Philemon to free his slave and allow him to return to Paul. This is a radical—and expensive—favor to ask. How does Paul support it?

Paul identifies Philemon in his opening greeting as "our dear friend and co-worker." (He also mentions Apphia "our sister" and Archippus "our fellow soldier," who may have been Philemon's wife and son, but they do not play a direct role in this story.) Since we have no other letters from Paul to individuals, it is impossible to know if these expressions of intimacy are unusual. It is clear, however, that Paul continues in the rest of the letter to emphasize and draw tight the network of relations that binds Paul, Philemon, and ultimately Onesimus together. He uses, for example, family terms to unite the trio: Paul and Philemon are "brothers" (vv. 7, 20), as are Philemon and Onesimus (v. 16). Paul is "father" to Onesimus his "child" (v. 10), and he has a similar relationship with Philemon, who owes Paul his "own self" (v. 19). In addition, Paul emphasizes the love that he has for Philemon (v. 1) and that Philemon has for the rest of the saints (vv. 5, 7). Later he will base his appeal to Philemon on this multidimensional love (v. 9) and extend it to include even the runaway slave (v. 16). Finally Paul greets Philemon as a co-worker, one who shares in the common work for the gospel. This too will become, as we will see, a subtle factor in Paul's appeal.

Out of this network, then, there emerge not only the common bonds of faith and love that unite all Christians, but also a special relationship between Paul, Philemon, and Onesimus that becomes the basis for a chain of actions that has Onesimus as the ultimate beneficiary. The three men are bound together in a complex debtor-creditor relationship. Philemon has received something precious from Paul—his very "self" (v. 19)—and thus is in debt to him. Onesimus has taken something valuable from Philemon (v. 18) and thus is in debt to *him*. Philemon, however, can discharge his debt to Paul by forgiving Onesimus's debt, accepting him back, and (if he does *more* than Paul asks) releasing him for service to the apostle. Thus a chain or circle of benefaction is forged here that is "closed" when Onesimus is free to return to Paul and serve the apostle on Philemon's behalf (v. 13). Paul's request for closure, however, is based explicitly on the *koinonia* (fellowship, partnership) he has with Philemon.

Paul speaks first of this *koinonia* in v. 6, an awkward and difficult verse to translate: "I pray that the sharing [*koinonia*] of your faith may become effective when you perceive all the good that we may do for Christ." This translation retains some of the awkwardness of the Greek, but what emerges rather clearly from the verse is the idea that Paul assumes a basic level of *koinonia* among Christians and expects concrete, practical results to come from it. Paul and Philemon are linked, however, by more than their common faith. Paul, as we have seen, is Philemon's spiritual "father." They are also "fellow workers," members of an inner circle devoted to the spread of the gospel (v. 24). Thus several layers of bonding lie behind and ground Paul's ultimate request: "So if you consider me your partner [*koinonos*], welcome him as you would welcome me" (v. 17).

In other more indirect ways Paul draws on these special relationships to motivate Philemon's response. He speaks of the joy he has already derived from Philemon (v. 7) and asks Philemon to act now in a way that will contribute further to that joy (v. 20). The New Revised Standard Version refers to "benefit" in this verse, suggesting the commercial language of Philippians, but the word, an unusual one in the New Testament, can also suggest joy: "Yea, brother, let me have joy of thee in the Lord" (KJV). Paul speaks of how Philemon has refreshed the hearts of the saints (v. 7) and asks him to act now in a way that will refresh Paul's heart also (v. 20).

Paul walks a delicate path in all of this. Like the ideal described in the Cynic letters, Paul insists that Philemon's response, whatever it is, must be freely given and not exacted under compulsion (v. 14). Yet he draws tight the net of relationships and the obligations they create, and he never really lets Philemon forget that he could, if he wished, simply insist that the thing be done (v. 8) and that he expects compliance, even if it is freely rendered (v. 21). He even shows a touch of the brazenness that characterized the Cynics, for when he closes his letter with a reference to a future visit, he is making it clear to Philemon that he will soon be present to see the results of his request.

The problem is that Paul obviously views what he is asking of Philemon as an extension of the gospel message. The faith and love that are due the Lord Jesus Christ must also be visible in one's relations with the saints (v. 5), among whom Onesimus now stands. Thus, in a sense, Philemon is under compulsion to do as Paul asks, especially if he is a co-worker for the gospel. Yet Paul also knows that the act must be freely done if it is to benefit the giver. In fact, Paul hints that Philemon *will* benefit from giving the gift that Paul requests, for as a result of accepting Onesimus back, and even more if he frees him, Philemon will receive not a slave but a "beloved brother." Thus, as in I Corinthians 9, Paul claims he has the right "in Christ" to command Philemon to do as he says, but he voluntarily waives this right in order to encourage Philemon voluntarily to waive *his* right to punish his slave and perhaps even his right of ownership over him as well (vv. 8-10).

CONCLUSIONS

What Cynics claimed by virtue of a special relationship with the gods, Paul claimed by virtue of his special apostolic status—the right to ask for and receive money for his apostolic work. But also out of this special status came his decision *not* to exercise this right lest it form an obstacle to these same apostolic labors. In this Paul seems to have been consistent: He did not ask for or accept money from a community in which he was actively working to establish a church. The basic reason he gives for this is his concern about hindering the forward movement of the gospel, whether by giving offense or by burdening fledgling churches. Once a church was established, however, he expected it to finance his travel to the next town. Clearly a concern for the gospel is paramount in Paul's expectations here as well. In fact, the action probably symbolized the base community's continuing participation in the gospel, and when this sense of participation was strong and healthy—and unchallenged by opponents—Paul could accept continued support from that community. Indeed, in these circumstances it became something of an obligation. Yet when this sort of support was not available, Paul willingly supported himself and *still* the gospel was served, for his labors illustrated the message of the cross. Paul was very flexible, and his flexibility was exclusively in the interest of the gospel and his churches.

In Corinth, however, Paul was challenged by rival apostles whose words and actions cast a shadow of suspicion on his financial arrangements. In this environment his flexibility became something of a liability, and to distinguish himself from impostors he retreated to a rigid position of no support. In Philippi, though, where this conflict was absent and where a sense of partnership prevailed, a cycle of benefaction propelled his ministry forward. Indeed, this partnership relationship seems to have been a principal criterion for asking for money just as the unimpeded advance of the gospel was its primary goal. Nevertheless, with the Philippians, the only church we know of that was committed to this level of support, Paul shows a concern to set limits on their financial responsibility, though a responsibility clearly it was.

When we turn to Philemon, this partnership relation is confirmed as a principal factor in Paul's practice of asking for money. When making his rather delicate and quite expensive request, Paul took great pains to establish the partnership that links him with Philemon. He also took pains to avoid explicit coercion even though his apostolic authority hovers constantly over the letter and its request. Ultimately, though, his appeal to Philemon rested not on authority but on the single phrase, "If you consider me your partner."

FOR FURTHER READING

There are a number of studies that help illuminate the nature and extent of Paul's missionary work. *The Social Pattern of Christian Groups in the First Century*, by E. A. Judge (London: Tyndale Press, 1960), and *Social Aspects of Early*

Christianity, by Abraham J. Malherbe (Baton Rouge, La.: Louisiana State University Press, 1977), establish the general social environment of Paul's mission. E. Earle Ellis's article, "Paul and His Co-Workers," *New Testament Studies* 17 (1970), pages 437-52, defines the extent and complexity of Paul's network of associates while Ronald F. Hock's book, *The Social Context of Paul's Ministry* (Philadelphia: Fortress Press, 1980), focuses on Paul's tentmaking and its implications for his missionary activity. The final chapter of Hock's book, "Tentmaking and Apostleship: The Debate at Corinth," is particularly relevant for our study.

Though focusing on various texts where Paul cites a saying of Jesus, David L. Dungan's book, *The Sayings of Jesus in the Churches of Paul* (Philadelphia: Fortress Press, 1971), contains a useful and thorough analysis of I Corinthians 9 and the issue of monetary support. Gerd Theissen's essay, "Legitimation and Subsistence," cited at the end of chapter 2, covers both I and II Corinthians and analyzes the role of financial arrangements in the conflict between Paul and his opponents. Several times I have referred to the work of Bengt Holmberg, whose book, *Paul and Power* (Philadelphia: Fortress Press, 1978), includes a substantial section on Paul's financial relations with his churches. An essay by E. A. Judge, "Cultural Conformity and Innovation in Paul," in *The Tyndale Bulletin* 35 (1984), pages 3-24, though somewhat abstract, is useful in defining the issues here, and I have alluded to it on page 71.

Victor P. Furnish's commentary on II Corinthians in the Anchor Bible Series (New York: Doubleday, 1984) contains excellent discussions of the relevant passages in that letter. Interpretation of II Corinthians is complicated by the fact that the letter in our canon may be composed of fragments of two or more letters, written over a period of rapid deterioration in the relationship between Paul and this church. Furnish's commentary defines this problem and describes the various "partition hypotheses" that have been proposed to explain the peculiar features of this letter. Most of the texts relevant for our study are found in a section of the letter (chaps. 10–13) that is recognized as a single unit, so I did not introduce the literary problem into the discussion.

Michael McDermott provides an overview of the biblical concept of *koinonia* in his article, "The Biblical Doctrine of *KOINONIA*," *Biblische Zeitschrift* 19 (1975), pages 64-77 and 219-33, while J. Paul Sampley focuses specifically on Paul's understanding in his book *Pauline Partnership in Christ* (Philadelphia: Fortress Press, 1980). Sampley, however, addresses the question from the perspective of the Latin concept of *societas,* which overlaps to some extent the Greek term *koinonia.*

Finally, Norman R. Petersen's book, *Rediscovering Paul* (Philadelphia: Fortress Press, 1985), provides a fresh, if somewhat complex, approach to Philemon that highlights the social structures undergirding the letter.

CHAPTER 4

PERSPECTIVES FROM PAUL, 2:
THE GREAT COLLECTION

*Only they would have us remember the poor, which
very thing I was eager to do.*
—*Galatians* 2:10 (RSV)

I f Paul showed a marked reluctance to ask for money for
his own support, at least while he was actively working in
a given community, he was tireless and aggressive about
promoting a particular collection destined for "the poor
among the saints at Jerusalem" (Rom. 15:26). In Galatians 2,
Paul indicates that he initially undertook the project at the
request of James, Cephas (Peter), and John. This request
took place at a meeting in Jerusalem, often referred to as the
Jerusalem or the Apostolic Council, which was probably held
in the year A.D. 48. Following this meeting Paul began the
phase of his apostolic work that led to the letters we have in
our canon, and when he wrote what turned out to be his last
letter, the letter to the Romans, he was still actively engaged
in making arrangements for this collection (Rom. 15:25-29).
Since Romans was probably written in the year A.D. 56, this
means that for *eight years* Paul worked to bring this project to
completion. What was its significance that Paul devoted so
much time and energy to it?

The Great Collection, as it is often called, must have been a
frequent topic in Paul's preaching, but we have only the
evidence of his letters to work with. Fortunately Paul refers to
it in several of these letters (Rom. 15:25-29; I Cor. 16:1-4;
Gal. 2:10), and two full chapters of II Corinthians (chaps. 8
and 9) are devoted to an extensive request for contributions.
From this material we should be able to discover the history

of the collection and its singular importance to Paul. Then we can explore II Corinthians 8–9 in some detail.

In these chapters we have a unique opportunity to listen directly to Paul asking his churches for money. How did he do it? What presuppositions about himself, about his communities, and about God did he bring to the task? What theological grounds did Paul use to justify his requests for contributions? What pragmatic arguments did he present to motivate his churches to give? What relationship did he see between these requests for money and his ministry as a whole? What constraints seem to operate on him? We need to listen carefully to Paul here, for his efforts on behalf of the Great Collection constitute our clearest picture of the fund-raising activities of the early church. Yet we must proceed with care, for this collection was unlike all others and we may misunderstand Paul if ever we forget that. What then *was* the Great Collection?

THE ORIGIN OF THE GREAT COLLECTION

To understand the nature of the Great Collection we need to go back to its point of origin, the Jerusalem Council of A.D. 48. There are actually two accounts of this council meeting in the New Testament, one in Acts 15 and the other in Galatians 2, and scholars have long noted that on many details these accounts do not agree. It is Paul's recollection of this event, however, on which we must focus, not only because he was an eyewitness to the events but also because only in Galatians do we find a reference to the collection. Acts does not mention it.

Paul wrote about the Jerusalem Council some years after the event as part of a spirited defense to the Galatians of the validity of his apostleship and of the law-free gospel that he proclaimed. Some people, probably conservative Jewish Christians, had visited Paul's Galatian churches after he left and insisted that the Gentile Christians there must be circumcised in order to complete their incorporation into the

Christian faith. Indeed, they seem to have suggested that Paul himself knew of the necessity of circumcision and had even been charged with that very message by the Jerusalem church. The only reason, they said, that Paul did not insist on it was to "please people" (Gal. 1:10), that is, to make the transition to Christianity easier for the Galatian converts.

Paul was quick to defend himself against these charges, and one aspect of his defense was to recount in exact detail ("In what I am writing to you, before God, I do not lie!" 1:20) all of his dealings with the Jerusalem church, including the historic meeting with apostles there some years earlier. The purpose of this review was to prove that at no time did Paul agree to a gospel that included circumcision and at no time did the Jerusalem apostles insist on it. Events at the council meeting were crucial to establishing this point.

After reviewing briefly his activities in the years immediately following his conversion, Paul described the council meeting in some detail. He says that he went up to Jerusalem "in response to a revelation" (2:2). The purpose of this trip was to present to the Jerusalem leadership of the church the understanding of the gospel that undergirded his missionary work among the Gentiles. Respect for the unity of the church required nothing less. Very quickly, according to Paul's account, the meeting focused on the issue of circumcision. Was this rite, symbolizing membership in the people of God, a necessary complement to faith? Some argued that it was, Paul insisted it was not, and he was absolutely clear about the outcome of this debate: "We did not submit to them even for a moment, so that the truth of the gospel might always remain with you [the Galatians]" (2:5). Then, because the point was very important to him, Paul added: "Those leaders [the Jerusalem apostles] contributed [RSV: added] nothing to me"; that is, they added no requirements to the admission of Gentiles into the church beyond their faith in Jesus Christ.

Paul thus stood firm in his insistence on the law-free gospel for Gentiles. Gentiles who accepted Jesus as Messiah did not have to take on the Jewish law or its requirement of circumcision. For their part, the Jewish Christians did not have to give up their law, but even for them it was no longer a principle of salvation. The result, though, was the creation of a two-pronged mission for Jews and for Gentiles, separate in form but equal in validity. Peter was to have charge of the mission to the Jews, who were free to keep the law, while Paul would continue his work with the Gentiles, who were free from it. Then all the apostles present—James, Cephas (Peter), and John from Jerusalem and Paul and Barnabas from the Gentile mission field—sealed the arrangement with "the right hand of fellowship" (2:9). Finally, almost as an afterthought, Paul mentions a parting request made by the Jerusalem apostles: "They asked only one thing, that we remember the poor, which was actually what I was eager to do."

The implications of this request are widely debated. It is clear, for example, from comments in some of Paul's other letters that although the phrase "remember the poor" sounds like a general admonition for almsgiving, Paul understood it to be a challenge to collect financial contributions from his churches for "the poor among the saints at Jerusalem" (Rom. 15:26; see I Cor. 16:1-4). But why just for this group? Was the economic situation of the Jerusalem church more precarious than that of the other churches? Was this church subject to greater danger of persecution because of its location?

The situation in Jerusalem was probably critical, but it was not unique. Indeed, Paul refers to the severe affliction and extreme poverty of the Macedonian churches as well, yet he asks *them* to contribute to the collection for Jerusalem (II Cor. 8:2). It is thus clearly not on economic grounds alone that the collection was destined for the Jerusalem church. Something more must have been at stake. Was it then, as some scholars have claimed, an assertion of control by the Jerusalem leaders, an obligation laid by them on Paul that seriously compromised the apostle's proud claim that they "added nothing to me" (RSV)? That, however, would make a mockery of the equality symbolized by the right hand of fellowship that was exchanged among the apostles. Others have argued that the collection was requested and undertaken with appreciation for its Jewish antecedents: the temple tax, for example, that guaranteed the symbolic participation of *all* the Jewish people in the temple sacrifices, or the "alms for Israel" that bonded "Godfearers," or Gentile sympathizers, with the Jewish religion. Possibly a number of factors were behind the request and probably the various participants each understood it somewhat differently. But while there is much that we cannot know about the original significance of this project, this much seems clear. The primary understanding of the collection must have been an act of benevolence, for Paul's later exhortations presuppose that a real economic need was being met (II Cor. 8:14; 9:12). But latent within the collection, both because of the setting in which the agreement arose and because of the symbolism it inherited from its Jewish antecedents, was a message of solidarity between the two wings of the Christian mission. Circumstances soon enhanced (in Paul's mind at least) this latent message and promoted the theological significance of the Great Collection.

By the time Paul wrote his letter to Rome, the theological dimension of the collection is clearly dominant in his thought. After expressing his hope of visiting the church in Rome on his way to Spain, Paul explains why he will be somewhat delayed:

> At present, however, I am going to Jerusalem in a ministry to the saints; for Macedonia and Achaia have been pleased to share their resources with the poor among the saints at Jerusalem. They were pleased to do this, and indeed they owe it to them; for if the Gentiles have come to share in their spiritual blessings, they ought also to be of service to them in material things. (Rom. 15:25-27)

It is striking that although Paul mentions the *poor* among the saints as the recipients of the contribution, he does not focus on their poverty or need as the motivating factor, but on the debt incurred by the Gentile Christians. He insists that the Gentile churches *owe* the Jerusalem saints this material gift because they have received from them, that is, from the Jewish Christians, a share in their spiritual blessings. The basic notion here is not almsgiving but reciprocity. But behind this reciprocity is an even more subtle message. Through it Paul professes the historical priority of the Jewish Christian church, which first received the spiritual blessings, but he also asserts that now these blessings have flowed, through missionaries like himself, from them to the Gentile world. In fact, the giving and receiving of material blessings now becomes a sign that this prior exchange of spiritual blessings has occurred. By contributing to the collection, the Gentiles acknowledge their debt to the Jewish Christians, but by accepting the collection the Jerusalem saints tacitly acknowledge the validity of the Gentile mission.

As Paul thus describes the collection in his letter to Rome, it is clear that the project has taken on overtones of the Jerusalem agreement. Through it each group recognizes the other as recipients of divine grace. This development is perhaps not surprising, since the collection had its inception at the Jerusalem meeting. What *is* surprising is that a few verses later Paul expresses some concern about the attitude of the Jerusalem saints toward the collection and asks the church in Rome to pray that it will be "acceptable" to them. Clearly the theological symbolism has not only eclipsed the charitable aspect of the gift, but it has also threatened to make the gift unacceptable to the very people who initially requested it. What has happened to make the theological dimension of the project not only so prominent in Paul's thought but also so problematical to the Jerusalem church?

The key to this may lie in an incident that brought to light the difficulty inherent in the Jerusalem agreement. As long as the Jewish and Gentile branches of the Christian movement were geographically separate, the separate arrangements concerning adherence to the Jewish law could work. At mixed gatherings, however, difficulties were bound to arise, especially if meals were involved, for the Jewish law had many strictures on food. And meals *were* involved in the Christian churches. The Lord's Supper, a central feature of Christian worship, involved not only the liturgical elements of the eucharist but an actual meal as well (I Cor. 11:17-34). But if the Jewish Christians followed the dietary regulations set out in the Jewish law code and the Gentile Christians did not, how could they sit down at table together? On the other hand, how could they *not* sit at table together if they were truly equal members of the body of Christ? Quite apart from its liturgical significance, eating together was a highly symbolic act and one not lightly undertaken—or ruptured.

This, however, is precisely what occurred at Antioch shortly after the council meeting. As Paul recounts it (Gal. 2:11-21), Peter initially acknowledged the freedom with regard to the law that both Jewish and Gentile Christians possessed. He ate with the Gentiles at Antioch. But when more conservative elements in the Jerusalem church objected, Peter reversed himself and withdrew from table fellowship with the Gentile Christians (2:12). Whatever words Peter may have used to justify this act, its symbolism was clear. If the Jewish Christians would not eat with their Gentile brothers and sisters, then the law, not grace, ruled their lives and they could not regard the Gentiles as truly equal members of the body of Christ. Small wonder, then, that Paul accused Peter of hypocrisy. Yet Peter seems to have persisted in his actions, for Paul would surely have mentioned it if he had persuaded Peter to return to table fellowship, and he does not. Here, then, was an event that not only ruptured the cordial relationship between the leaders of the Jewish and Gentile missions but also seemed to undermine the very theological basis of the two-pronged mission.

It was under these circumstances that the latent theological significance of the collection as well as concern about its acceptance grew in Paul's mind. This act of charity became for him a way of repairing the strained relationship between the two wings of the church. The Gentiles would demonstrate through their willing participation in the gift their sense of solidarity with the Jewish Christians, and the latter would in turn reaffirm by their acceptance of the gift the validity and vitality of Paul's law-free mission to the Gentiles. The collection became a symbol for Paul of the right hand of fellowship *(koinonia)* originally extended to him by the Jerusalem apostles and later, at Antioch, partially withdrawn. This idea of fellowship between the two branches of the Christian mission as well as between their leaders was so important a component of the collection that when Paul wrote to Rome he actually called the collection a *koinonia,* a fact English translations of the letter are unable to communicate.

This symbolism is present not only in Paul's letter to the Romans, but also in II Corinthians, which was probably written only a short time before. The volatile situation in Corinth, however, contributed another, distinctive layer of significance to the collection. Thus before we can listen adequately to the requests for contributions that Paul makes in that letter, we need to review some of the developments in Corinth. Questions about the integrity of II Corinthians, however, make this survey somewhat complex.

DEVELOPMENTS IN CORINTH

I have already alluded in chapter 3 to the difficulty one encounters when trying to interpret II Corinthians. The last four chapters of the letter are vastly different in tone and content from the earlier chapters. In 11:1-11, for example, Paul is hurt, defensive, and sarcastic in his comments to the church, while in 7:13-16 he speaks warmly of his confidence, pride, and joy in them. Because of differences like this, many scholars are convinced that at least two different letters have been combined to form what is now II Corinthians. Indeed, as many as four or five letters may be represented, for some scholars maintain that chapters 8 and 9 were originally independent as well. This raises real problems for the interpreter. How many letters are represented? What are the probable limits of the different letters? What was their original sequence and context?

Many scholars identify the emotionally charged final chapters (II Cor. 10–13) with a "tearful letter" that Paul mentions: "For I wrote you out of much distress and anguish of heart and with many tears, not to cause you pain, but to let you know the abundant love that I have for you" (II Cor. 2:4). According to this hypothesis, chapters 10–13 were written first and chapters 1–7 derive from a letter written after the apostle was reconciled with his church (II Cor. 7:6-13). Others, however, find problems with this reconstruction. Chapters 10–13 seem more angry than tearful to them, so the "tearful letter" must be missing. If that is the case, then II Corinthians could reflect the actual unfolding of events. Following the (missing) "tearful letter" there was a reconciliation between Paul and the church during which he wrote II Corinthians 1–7. Later, however, the relationship deteriorated again, and chapters 10–13 were written during this troubled period. Where do chapters 8 and 9, with their extensive requests for contributions, fit into these scenarios? Some think that because these chapters are similar in content yet somewhat inconsistent in argument, they must originally have been two separate letters, separate from each other as well as from the other letters Paul wrote to this church. Others disagree, finding enough points of continuity between chapters 8 and 9 and the preceding chapters to posit a single letter encompassing all of the first nine chapters. On only one point is there general agreement. It is unlikely that either request for money, chapter 8 or chapter 9, was written when the apostle was in the hurt and embittered mood reflected in chapters 10–13.

Scholars are obviously deeply divided on these issues, which are far too complex to explore in more detail here. Yet they are of obvious importance for our investigation of chapters 8 and 9. Whether these chapters were originally separate or united does not dramatically affect our analysis, but it is important to know whether Paul's requests for money preceded or followed his conflict with the Corinthian church. Certainty on these issues is not possible, but the argument that chapters 10–13 were written *before* chapters 1–8 (9) seems slightly more persuasive to me. This produces the following sequence of events.

After Paul wrote I Corinthians, rival apostles arrived in Corinth, significantly altering the dynamics of that community and its relationship to Paul. We have already discussed these apostles and their disruptive effect on the community. Among other things, they seem to have disrupted the community's participation in the Great Collection. Paul had obviously discussed the collection with the Corinthians while he was staying with them and he mentions the topic again in I Corinthians. His comments in that letter seem to indicate that the Corinthians had only modest enthusiasm for the project and perhaps a concern about how it was to be delivered (I Cor. 16:1-4), but there is no evidence of serious tension over it. This, however, changed dramatically after the new apostles arrived. In addition to belittling Paul's refusal to accept recompense for his apostolic labors, they also seem to have suggested that Paul actually used the Great Collection as a means of secretly enriching himself. Paul responded to these events by writing a letter (chaps. 10–13) that expressed his hurt and outrage:

> Let it be assumed that I did not burden you. Nevertheless (you say) since I was crafty, I took you in by deceit. Did I take advantage of you through any of those whom I sent to you? I urged Titus to go, and sent the brother with him. Titus did not take advantage of you, did he? Did we not conduct ourselves with the same spirit? Did we not take the same steps?
> (II Cor. 12:16-18)

The suspicions Paul addresses here were apparently strong enough to halt all preparations for the collection. When Paul was later reconciled with this church, he worked energetically to revitalize their commitment to this project, but a residue of suspicion still seemed to linger over the collection. Thus even in his letter of reconciliation (chaps. 1–8 or 1–9) he protested, "We intend that no one should blame us about this generous gift that we are administering" (II Cor. 8:20), and to this end he made arrangements for several delegates, one of them appointed by the churches, to accompany and supervise the collection (8:16-24). The lingering effects of the crisis are visible in another way as well, for in the aftermath of this emotionally charged event, Paul seemed to make the Corinthians' participation in the collection a test of their restored confidence in him. The evidence for this is somewhat ambiguous, which may indicate Paul's reluctance to take this significant step, but it is evocative.

In the crisis generated by the rival apostles, not only was Paul's love for the church called into question ("And why? Because I do not love you? God knows I do!" 11:11), but also the church's love for Paul ("If I love you more, am I to be loved less?" 12:15). When Paul wrote after his reconciliation with the church, his relief at their restored "zeal" for him is evident:

> But God, who consoles the downcast, consoled us by the arrival of Titus, and not only by his coming, but also by the consolation with which he was consoled about you, as he told us of your longing, your mourning, your zeal for me, so that I rejoiced still more. (II Cor. 7:6-7)

Nevertheless, when Paul turned to the topic of the collection, he raised again the question of the depth of their commitment to him, but he did so subtly, aware, perhaps, of the potentially treacherous path he was taking.

Paul began his discussion of the collection by presenting

the participation of the Macedonian churches—which would include Philippi, Thessalonica, and probably Beroea—as a model, or a goad, for the Corinthians. He noted that the Macedonians "gave themselves first to the Lord *and, by the will of God, to us*" (8:5, emphasis added). The final phrase has puzzled some commentators, who find it surprising that Paul would speak in the same breath of giving oneself to Christ and to him, yet the Corinthians' allegiance to him had long been on Paul's mind (7:5-13). A few verses later he praises the Corinthians for a number of things in which they excel: their faith, their eloquence, their understanding, and their zeal. Then he concludes the list with a rather surprising reference to "our love for you" (8:7). One would have expected in this list of the *Corinthians'* virtues a reference to "your love for us" instead. Indeed, some Greek manuscripts and most English translations, including the Revised Standard Version, do have these more logical words. The New Revised Standard Version, however, restores the more difficult—and probably the more original—wording, "our love for you." Paul says they excelled in his love for them, but if the early manuscripts are correct, he was apparently silent here on the question of their love for him. In the very next verse, though, Paul asserts that he has mentioned the zeal of the Macedonians, who gave themselves to him, in order to test their love. Love for whom? Paul does not explicitly say. Certainly participation in the collection as an act of charity would reflect their basic Christian love as well as their special love and esteem for the Jerusalem church. But did Paul view it as a test to confirm the Corinthians' love for him as well? Given the context of the remark, it seems likely that he did, and he closes the chapter with another ambiguous exhortation: "Therefore openly before the churches, show them the proof of your love" (v. 24).

In summary: After the Jerusalem Council, where Paul accepted a collection for the poor in Jerusalem as his special charge, several events occurred that transformed the significance of this project. Though the collection was perhaps originally just an expression of the concern for the underprivileged that characterized Christianity from the start, first the episode in Antioch and then the crisis in Corinth bestowed on it new layers of meaning. Indeed, by the time Paul wrote to the Corinthians to rekindle their flagging zeal for the collection, the project was quite loaded with theological value. Still, one is unprepared for the extraordinary way Paul discusses the project in chapters 8 and 9.

ASKING FOR MONEY: II CORINTHIANS 8–9

The first thing one notices in these chapters is the rich theological texture of the language that Paul uses to describe, define, and promote the collection. We have already discussed the importance of the concept of *koinonia* for this project. Here a number of other theologically loaded terms are added to the discussion. The Greek word *charis*, for example, is very prominent in these chapters. Here, as elsewhere, Paul uses this word, which basically means "gift" or "favor," to convey the central point of his theology— divine grace. He *also* uses the word here, however, to define the collection (8:6, 7, 19). Here, too, *diakonia*, which means "service" or "ministry," becomes an epithet for the collection (8:4; 9:1, 12, 13), as does *eulogia* (9:5, 6), which means literally "blessing" or "praise." Even *leitourgia*, a term which usually refers to priestly or cultic service but originally designated, as we have seen, the nearly obligatory donations of upper classes to public service projects, is applied to this project (9:12). Not only are these terms abundant in these two chapters, but Paul often plays one term off another, or plays with different meanings of a term, always weaving them so deeply into his argument that the theological dimensions of his request cannot be disengaged from the request itself.

All of this makes the passage exceptionally difficult to translate. Indeed, it is nearly impossible to translate it in a way that preserves all the theological overtones of the language and at the same time retains the intelligibility of the argument itself. Perhaps the only way to see how Paul works these theological ideas into his request is to go through his argument step by step and highlight its significant features.

Overflowing Grace

> We want you to know, brothers and sisters, about the grace of God that has been granted to the churches of Macedonia; for during a severe ordeal of affliction, their abundant joy and their extreme poverty have overflowed in a wealth of generosity on their part. For, as I can testify, they voluntarily gave according to their means, and even beyond their means, begging us earnestly for the privilege of sharing in this ministry to the saints—and this, not merely as we expected; they gave themselves first to the Lord and, by the will of God, to us, so that we might urge Titus that, as he had already made a beginning, so he should also complete this generous undertaking among you. Now as you excel in everything—in faith, in speech, in knowledge, in utmost eagerness, and in our love for you—so we want you to excel also in this generous undertaking. (II Cor. 8:1-7)

Paul's first step toward reawakening the Corinthians' zeal for the collection was to report to them the response of their neighbors to the north. After describing the difficult circumstances in Macedonia and the generous and spontaneous giving of the churches there, Paul makes a surprising statement: He concludes that he should urge Titus to complete the project among the Corinthians (8:6). Paul reacted to the *Macedonians'* generosity by sending Titus to work on the collection *in Corinth!* That is not, on the face of it, an obvious response. Clearly he saw more in this event than meets our eye; what must have amazed Paul was the miraculous quality of the Macedonians' actions. Though themselves in a situation of affliction and poverty, they viewed the opportunity to contribute to the collection not as a burden but as a gift (*charis,* translated "privilege" in v. 4) and responded with willing zeal. Such a response could itself only be a gift of God, an outpouring of God's own grace in the church (v. 1). Thus Paul turned immediately to the Corinthian church, confident that this outpouring of grace would spread even to that troubled community. A few verses later Paul describes Titus as undertaking the trip to Corinth with the same zeal as the Macedonians had displayed (vv. 16-17), further evidence, it seems, of God's grace *(charis)* moving inexorably toward that city. One thus gets a sense of the powerful workings of God's grace, how it overcame the obstacles in Macedonia and now was overflowing into Corinth to challenge the obstacles that had arisen there.

Charis is the key word here, but it conveys various meanings. Paul uses it first to refer to God's activity in Macedonia (v. 1) and then to that church's participation in the collection (v. 4), indicating that one is rooted in the other. By verses 6-7, he calls the collection itself a *charis* (NRSV: "generous undertaking"), extending the word chain one more evocative step. God's grace, says Paul, is bound up with this collection-gift. Participation in the collection is not simply a responsibility urged on the churches, it is at one and the same time God's gift to them. Paul thus aligns his request for participation with a list of things in which the Corinthians excel but which are, at the same time, spiritual gifts that they have been given: faith, speech, knowledge, and zeal *(see* I Cor. 1:4-8; 12:8-11). It is clear in all of this that it is not the monetary contribution *per se* that Paul celebrates in Macedonia and urges in Corinth, but the giving of *self* that the gift symbolizes. Thus he can say that zealous participation in the concrete collection-gift is not merely one good deed among many, but an act that confirms the transforming presence of more intangible spiritual gifts. As a concrete symbol of self-giving, participation in the collection can even be described as the culmination of spiritual growth: "Now as you excel in everything—in faith, in speech, in knowledge, in utmost eagerness, and in our love for you—so we want you to excel also in this generous undertaking" (v. 7).

Zeal and Reciprocity

> I do not say this as a command, but I am testing the genuineness of your love against the earnestness of others. For you know the generous act of our Lord Jesus Christ, that though he was rich, yet for your sakes he became poor, so that by his poverty you might become rich. And in this matter I am giving my advice: it is appropriate for you who began last year not only to do something but even to desire to do something—now finish doing it, so that your eagerness may be matched by completing it according to your means. For if the eagerness is there, the gift is acceptable according to what one has—not according to what one does not have. I do not mean that there should be relief for others and pressure on you, but it is a question of a fair balance between your present abundance and their need, so that their abundance may be for your need, in order that there may be a fair balance. As it is written, "The one who had much did not have too much, and the one who had little did not have too little."
> (8:8-15)

Because of the symbolic value of the collection as a sign to the Jerusalem church of the validity of the Gentile mission and of the solidarity of the two branches of the church, it was vitally important that contributions be given in a generous spirit (v. 2) and, of course, that they be given voluntarily. The collection could hardly function as an effective sign of partnership if it were a miserly amount or given under compulsion. Thus Paul hastens to say that he does not urge this "as a command" (v. 8). Indeed, if participation in the collection is itself a gift, as Paul has argued, he *cannot* command participation. Yet he does present this "generous undertaking" for others as an appropriate mode of response to the grace that Christ manifested in his own self-giving. This again highlights the giving of *self* as the theological heart of the collection.

The centrality of this aspect of the collection seems to be confirmed by the odd sequence of phrases that Paul uses in verse 10. Whereas one would expect as the natural sequence a comment like, "You began *not only to desire something but also to do it*" (*see*, e.g., Rom. 7:18*b*), Paul says instead that the Corinthians began *not only to do something but also to desire it*. This comment suggests that the orientation of the heart—the self—surpasses in importance the execution of the deed, for it is *zeal* or *desire* that confirms the presence of God's grace within them. Indeed, as Nils Dahl has noted, the collection takes on an almost sacramental quality in Paul's thought insofar as zeal for it becomes "a visible sign of invisible grace," tangible evidence of God's love in their hearts.

The collection is also, Paul continues to insist, a component of the reciprocity that reflects and sustains the mutual partnership of Jewish and Gentile Christians in God's work of grace. This is clearer in the Greek text than in English translations, for the Greek refers to their contributions as coming "out of equality . . . in order that there might be equality" (v. 14). The equality effected by God's grace is thus the basis for Paul's requests for contributions and the reason that he states as his goal a level of material equality. Equality begets equality, not new inequities, and he wants to symbolize concretely the new spiritual reality. On two levels Paul thus encourages—but does not command—participation in the collection here. Contributions to this collection-gift are an appropriate response to God's grace-gift, and they effect a degree of equality that symbolizes on the material level the equal standing of all members of the church in this divine grace.

The remaining verses of this chapter are devoted to arrangements for the actual collection of the funds that the Corinthians have prepared. These arrangements show the pains Paul takes to avoid any hint of unscrupulous behavior and seem to reflect Paul's earlier crisis with this church. It is in the next chapter that he renews his exhortations concerning the gathering of these funds.

Theological Echoes

> Now it is not necessary for me to write you about the ministry to the saints, for I know your eagerness, which is the subject of my boasting about you to the people of Macedonia, saying that Achaia has been ready since last year; and your zeal has stirred up most of them. But I am sending the brothers in order that our boasting about you may not prove to have been empty in this case, so that you may be ready, as I said you would be; otherwise, if some Macedonians come with me and find that you are not ready, we would be humiliated—to say nothing of you—in this undertaking. So I thought it necessary to urge the brothers to go on ahead to you, and arrange in advance for this bountiful gift that you have promised, so that it may be ready as a voluntary gift and not as an extortion. (9:1-5)

Paul's shift in tactic is odd here, especially if chapter 9 was originally part of a letter that also contained chapter 8. Having praised the Macedonians' zeal in order to prod the Corinthians into participation (8:1-7), he now says that he uses the *Corinthians'* zeal to stir up the Macedonians' interest (9:1-5). This is a surprising revelation. A reader would not have guessed from chapter 8 that the Macedonians needed any prodding at all. Nor would the reader of that chapter suspect that the region of Achaia, which includes Corinth, had been ready since last year! Various solutions to this puzzle have been proposed, including the pervasive opinion that these chapters were originally separate letters, sent at different times and perhaps even to different churches. On the other hand, the verses quoted above continue the arrangements for the collection that were begun in chapter 8, so an argument can be made for the unity of the chapters as well. Our focus on Paul's methods of asking for money is not, however, radically affected by this issue.

Whether originally one letter or two, Paul clearly encouraged a rivalry between the two regions in order to promote the collection in both. When Paul wrote these verses, however, the tactic was threatening to backfire. His boast about the Corinthians had been premature; they had *not* completed their preparations for the collection, yet the Macedonians, spurred by Paul's exaggerated report of the Corinthians' efforts, had. Moreover, if the Corinthian church were not galvanized into immediate action, the Macedonians would soon discover this embarrassing situation. Thus Paul, fearing humiliation both for himself and for his church, renewed his efforts on behalf of the collection. Yet, as before, his theological argument soon eclipsed his very human concerns.

In chapter 8 Paul described the collection as a gift *(charis)* and as a partnership *(koinonia)* with the Jewish Christians. In verse 4 of that chapter, Paul brought both of these rich terms together and added a third as well: *diakonia.* (English translations are unable to convey adequately the complex interplay of theological ideas that this creates.) Now in the opening verse of chapter 9 he refers to the collection again as a ministry or service *(diakonia)*. The word *diakonia* recalls the original significance of the collection as an act of charitable assistance or service to the poorer Jerusalem church, but in the Pauline letters the term refers to the ministerial office of the church as well. Thus Paul speaks of his own ministry or service of reconciliation (II Cor. 5:18), of the "servant" ministry of Apollos (I Cor. 3:5), of Phoebe (Rom. 16:1), and even of Christ (Rom. 15:8). Indeed, ministry can take many forms, as Paul himself explicitly says (I Cor. 12:5), and participation in the collection is clearly one of them. This ministry, though, assumes a special liturgical quality that adds a new dimension to the collection. Paul suggests this later in the chapter by linking the term *diakonia* (ministry, service) with *leitourgia* (service, liturgy) and describing it as ushering in a flood of thanksgivings to God: "For the rendering of this ministry [literally: "the ministry *(diakonia)* of this liturgy *(leitourgia)*"] not only supplies the needs of the saints but also *overflows with many thanksgivings to God*" (II Cor. 9:12, emphasis added). Giving to others thus glorifies God

(v. 13), and an act of charity is thereby transformed into an act of worship.

Paul also describes the Corinthians' contribution as a *eulogia* (blessing) in verse 5. English translations obscure the theological dimension of this term somewhat by rendering it "bounty" or "bountiful gift," but overtones of the more familiar meaning of the word, "blessing," are present in Paul's thought as well. It is not simply that their contributions will provide a blessing to the Jerusalem church, but through their actions *God* will provide a blessing to the Jerusalem church and to the Corinthians as well. This can happen, however, only if the gift is freely and generously given. Paul develops these ideas in the next verses.

A Chain of Benefaction

> The point is this: the one who sows sparingly will also reap sparingly, and the one who sows bountifully will also reap bountifully. Each of you must give as you have made up your mind, not reluctantly or under compulsion, for God loves a cheerful giver. And God is able to provide you with every blessing in abundance, so that by always having enough of everything, you may share abundantly in every good work. As it is written, "He scatters abroad, he gives to the poor; his righteousness endures forever." He who supplies seed to the sower and bread for food will supply and multiply your seed for sowing and increase the harvest of your righteousness. You will be enriched in every way for your great generosity, which will produce thanksgiving to God through us; for the rendering of this ministry not only supplies the needs of the saints but also overflows with many thanksgivings to God. Through the testing of this ministry you glorify God by your obedience to the confession of the gospel of Christ and by the generosity of your sharing with them and with all others, while they long for you and pray for you because of the surpassing grace of God that he has given you. Thanks be to God for his indescribable gift! (9:6-15)

The first point Paul makes in these verses is that the gift must be given with an open heart and hand, a point he has made before (8:3). We have already indicated some of the reasons for Paul's concern for a free and willing gift. Here another emerges. Three times Paul emphasizes that God will provide to the giver (9:8, 10, 11). Each time, however, the providing is presented not as a *reward* for the giver's generosity but as an *enabler* of it, not as a result of generosity but as a source for continuing generosity. The New English Bible states this point succinctly: "You will always be rich enough to be generous" (9:11). Though convinced that God would provide for them richly, Paul does not allow crass materialism to emerge as a motivating factor. Whatever the Corinthians received would simply enable more generosity.

The Corinthians are thus a link in a chain of benefaction, agents of God's generosity. As such they must reflect this divine generosity in their own giving, for they are to be not only recipients of it but also conduits for it. Grace is not static. God's gifts to the Corinthians will overflow into abundance for the Jerusalem saints (v. 8). Indeed, God's gifts to Corinth will overflow back to God through the "many thanksgivings" that their generosity will generate. Grace here reveals its true nature, for it is the essence of grace to overflow any situation or vessel into which it has been poured (Rom. 5:15-21). It will overflow the Macedonian vessel into Corinth. It will overflow the Corinthian vessel as contributions for Jerusalem, and overflowing finally the Jerusalem vessel, it will return to God as undiminished thanksgiving and praise. Paul signals that the process has already begun: "Thanks *(charis)* be to God for his indescribable gift!" (II Cor. 9:15).

AFTERMATH

Paul's zeal for the collection is clear; its ultimate fate, however, is almost completely hidden to us. We know nothing, for example, about the size of the gift Paul was able to send to Jerusalem. In a way, that is appropriate, since Paul repeatedly insisted that it was the will to give and not the amount that reflected the presence of God's grace. But we do not even know with certainty which communities ultimately displayed that will. In I Corinthians 16:1, Paul indicates that the Galatian churches had begun to gather monies for the collection, but when he describes the project to the Romans, he mentions only Macedonia and Achaia as participants. What happened to the Galatian effort? We don't know. Did Corinth eventually join the other Achaian churches in making a contribution? We don't know.

Acts is of no help to us here, for this book is completely silent on the question of the collection. This is perhaps the biggest surprise of all: that this project, which came to symbolize the validity of the Gentile mission, the unity of the church, and the mysterious workings of God's grace, should go unmentioned in the earliest story of the church. There may be some faint memory of it in the report of Paul's extensive entourage on the final trip to Jerusalem (Acts 20:4), for we know that Paul's arrangements for the collection included several delegates from the churches (I Cor. 16:3; II Cor. 8:18-23). Another echo may be found in Acts 24:17, where Paul's final trip to Jerusalem is described as motivated by the desire "to bring alms to my nation." But alms for the *nation* are quite different from contributions for the poor among the saints in Jerusalem, and nowhere does Acts record the acceptance by the Jerusalem church of a monetary gift culminating and symbolizing Paul's efforts among the Gentiles. Does this mean that the fears Paul expressed about the collection's "acceptability" to the saints were realized? We don't know, but the silence of Acts is troubling.

CONCLUSIONS

Nowhere do we find a more complex picture of the early church's practice of asking for money than in Paul's comments on the Great Collection. Suspect personal motives and flagrant psychological manipulation stand side by side with arguments of great theological depth and sensitivity. So subtle are these arguments that English translations are consistently unable to capture them. Paul seems originally to have asked his churches to contribute to the collection in response to a charitable request from his apostolic colleagues. His motive would thus have been to fulfill the service ministry to which he and all Christians were called. As more layers of meaning were added to the project, however, the motives for Paul's involvement changed as well. By the time of his final preparations for its delivery to Jerusalem, its meaning and his motives were considerably more complex.

Paul asked for contributions, for example, because he had been entrusted with the message of grace, and the collection had become for him not just part of that message but part of that grace. Participation in the collection was grace made real in the lives of the communities, a sign of the transformed quality of their lives and a conduit to others of that transforming grace. Because of this identification with grace, external compulsion was unacceptable. Nor should it be necessary, for if Paul's churches had truly experienced God's grace, they would, like the Macedonians, voluntarily—and eagerly—respond. Grace, then, had its own dynamic that would carry the collection along.

This does not mean, however, that Paul's role was entirely passive. Indeed, the intensity of Paul's requests almost implied a command, though that was held in check by his insistence on voluntary participation. In II Corinthians he even urged participation in the collection as a test of the Corinthians' love for him, yet as the argument unfolds it becomes clear that the collection is even more an opportunity to realize and reveal the love and grace of God present in them. Thus Paul asked for contributions out of a sense of the churches' indebtedness. Those who have received a gift are expected to make some return to the giver. When the giver is God and the gift is grace, one way to do this is to convey the gift to others. For Paul, however, spiritual and material manifestations of the gift are interchangeable, so Paul called on his communities to respond to God's grace by making material contributions to relieve the needs of others.

Paul also saw this indebtedness on another plane. The Gentile Christians were in debt to the Jewish Christians for the gospel, and they could repay that spiritual debt through their material contributions. The reciprocity of this exchange was further rooted in a sense of partnership between the two wings of Christianity, and Paul asked for contributions to symbolize and solidify this sense of shared goals and equal worth. The collection thus became a vehicle for conveying a message about the unity of the church.

Finally Paul asked for contributions because giving is not only an act of service, it is also an act of worship, a vehicle for returning thanks and praise to God. Though the base motives of the real world occasionally intruded, as when Paul turned the collection into a test of the Corinthians' love for him, these were soon overwhelmed and obscured by the theological significance that Paul saw in the event. Indeed, the collection became a summary, even an embodiment, of the Christian message: grace, fellowship, unity, service, and worship.

What factors constrained or controlled Paul's requests for contributions? The theological implications of the collection were so significant that Paul's words in II Corinthians have an insistent, even an urgent quality. Moreover, Paul used some problematical techniques. He pitted community against community and seemed to misrepresent the efforts of one to provoke the other to greater participation. He even seemed to make participation into a loyalty test for Corinth. At the same time the theological dimensions of the project provide constraints to these excesses. It is ultimately a matter of grace, and grace cannot be compelled. It is also a matter of fellowship and equality, not enrichment of one group at the expense of the other. And Paul made it absolutely clear that this request for money into which he had poured so much time and energy was entirely and exclusively for the benefit of others. Finally, we should not forget that Paul was in fundamental theological disagreement with the leaders of the Jerusalem church (Gal. 2:14-21), yet it was to these men that he planned to turn over the entire proceeds of the collection.

There is an ecumenical vision here and a depth of faith and trust that transcend and transform any petty motives that may occasionally have intruded. Paul trusted that the collection would further God's purposes. On the basis of that trust he asked for money and undertook the dangerous voyage to Jerusalem. If grace propelled the collection, it was faith and trust that sustained it. Paul made some questionable decisions about the collection that may have exacerbated his churches' suspicions and their reluctance to participate. For its part, the Jerusalem church may have been prevented by political exigencies or narrowness of theological vision from accepting the money that Paul brought. None of this, however, diminishes Paul's insight into the theological and ethical aspects of asking for money within the church.

FOR FURTHER READING

Though much of the research on the Great Collection has been published in German, there are several fine studies available in English. The most extensive of these is *The Collection: A Study in Paul's Strategy* by Keith F. Nickle (Studies in Biblical Theology 48; London: SCM Press, 1966). Nickle provides careful analyses of the relevant New Testament texts and the possible Jewish antecedents of the collection. In his treatment of its theological dimensions, he discusses various points mentioned here, but he also argues that the project had eschatological significance for Paul. This thesis, too detailed to present here, is intriguing but highly inferential, and Nickle must offer elaborate explanations of why Paul does not explicitly mention this aspect of the collection if it was so important to him.

Somewhat briefer discussions of the Great Collection can be found in other works as well. At the end of chapter 3, I mentioned the work of Sampley *(Pauline Partnership in Christ)* and Holmberg *(Paul and Power)*. Sampley devotes one chapter of his book to Paul's view of the Jerusalem Conference and suggests there that from the outset, because of their different backgrounds, Paul and the Jerusalem apostles understood the significance of "giving the right hand" in quite different ways. Such a difference radically affected the way they understood the collection as well. Holmberg presents a similar argument and emphasizes the element of obligation in the original request that could have signaled the supremacy of the Jerusalem church. Nils A. Dahl's study, "Paul and Possessions," found in his collection of essays entitled *Studies in Paul* (Minneapolis, Minn.: Augsburg, 1977), is a more general survey of Paul's judgments concerning material goods. He makes a number of comments, however, about the collection and contributes the insight into the sacramental quality that Paul attributes to the act of giving. Oscar Cullmann, on the other hand, has focused on the message of reciprocity and equality that the collection conveys and makes that the basis for an ecumenical suggestion he develops in a little book entitled *Message to Catholics and Protestants* (Grand Rapids: Wm. B. Eerdmans Publishing Co., 1959).

There are a number of fine commentaries on II Corinthians. Two in particular should be mentioned not only because they present particularly good discussions of the relevant chapters but also because they are based on quite different presuppositions about the relationship of chapters 8 and 9 to the rest of the letter. Hans Dieter Betz's commentary in the Hermeneia series (Philadelphia: Fortress Press, 1985) is devoted exclusively to II Corinthians 8–9. He focuses on the rhetorical dimensions of these chapters, treating them as two separate letters originally addressed to different audiences after the resolution of Paul's crisis with the Corinthian church. Furnish's commentary, cited in chapter 3, covers the entire text of II Corinthians and treats chapters 8 and 9 as part of a single conciliatory letter comprising chapters 1 through 9. Furnish further assumes that this letter *precedes* the crisis with the church that prompted Paul to write chapters 10–13. Both Betz and Furnish thus differ somewhat from my own evaluation of the chapters and should be consulted for the different perspectives they provide.

CHAPTER 5

PERSPECTIVES FROM ACTS:
MONEY AND POWER

All who believed were together and
had all things in common.
—*Acts 2:44*

Ｗe need to consider a brief episode in the book of
Acts before we conclude our survey of what the
New Testament has to say about the practice of
asking for money. Acts, written as a sequel to the Gospel of
Luke, tells the story of the early church in a way that is rich
with theological overtones. (Since the same author wrote
both Luke and Acts, we will follow the usual convention of
calling the author "Luke," but see above, page 59.) One
aspect of this story, the communal life-style described in the
quotation above, is of particular interest to us here, for
implicit in this life-style is a powerful request for money.
Insofar as Luke suggests that sharing of possessions was
strongly encouraged—or even mandated—by the church, he
suggests that those who embraced the Christian faith were
placed under a strong and perhaps absolute moral impera-
tive to give. He even mentions the dreadful fates of Ananias
and Sapphira to underscore the seriousness of this impera-
tive. Thus while explicit requests for money do not appear in
Luke's description of the early Christian church, the
communal life-style of this church imposed a request on its
members that could not easily be ignored.

There is some debate over whether community of goods
actually existed in the early church and, if it did, how
rigorously and how long it was practiced. Skeptics note that
after Luke gives a general description of the practice in the

Jerusalem church, he mentions the actions of a certain Barnabas as if they were exceptional rather than the common rule: "There was a Levite, a native of Cyprus, Joseph, to whom the apostles gave the name Barnabas (which means 'son of encouragement'). He sold a field that belonged to him, then brought the money, and laid it at the apostles' feet" (Acts 4:36-37). Moreover, the practice is not mentioned in later chapters of Acts, so it appears at best to be an isolated episode in the story of the church. On the other hand, the *Didache* seems to reflect some form of community of goods at the end of the first century, for although its instructions on almsgiving and support of traveling prophets presuppose some private control of possessions, the document also says,

> Thou shalt not turn away the needy, but shalt share everything with thy brother, and shalt not say that it is thine own, for if you are sharers in the imperishable, how much more in the things which perish? (*Did.* 4.8)

The historical reliability of the description of the life-style of the early community is thus difficult to assess. While the picture in Acts is obviously idealized, it may rest on actual episodes of sharing possessions, but how much this was the case can no longer be recovered. But if we cannot reconstruct the actual historical circumstances of the early church accurately enough to work with, we can evaluate the function of the comments on sharing possessions within the narrative of Acts. That is, quite apart from questions of historical reliability, we can look at Luke's story of the early church *as a story* and we can consider the social and theological dimensions of the practice of community of goods that are suggested by this story. Thus we need to look at the sociological shape of the community as Luke describes it, the theological shape he has given to the narrative, and the themes that gain prominence in it. When we are able to situate the passages about the community of goods within the interplay of these themes and in this social world, an important aspect of asking for money is conveyed by these texts.

There is, however, a problem. Luke-Acts is a very complex work and there are many ways that we could begin. We could, for example, begin with the role of the disciples and develop the correspondence between the radical demands of discipleship presented in the gospel and the community of goods advocated in Acts. We could also begin with the concern for the poor that dominates Luke and explore the community of goods as the expression of a social world that embraces that concern. Instead, I would like to follow the lead that Luke T. Johnson has established in his book, *The Literary Function of Possessions in Luke-Acts,* and show how the descriptions of the community of goods in the early church can be viewed in terms of the issue of communal authority—in particular, the authority of the apostles that is rooted in their election (Acts 10:41) and nourished by the power they received from on high (Luke 24:49).

COMMUNITY OF GOODS: AN IDYLLIC PICTURE

In the opening verses of Acts, the author establishes the continuity between this volume and the Gospel of Luke. First he summarizes very briefly the contents of the gospel ("all that Jesus did and taught") and then he picks up the story where the gospel left off. He does this in such a way, however, that the two volumes overlap slightly and the points of overlap define points of emphasis in the narrative. Thus the gospel closes with a scene in which the departing Jesus announces to the eleven remaining apostles (the defection of Judas has diminished by one the ranks of the twelve) that repentance and forgiveness are to be preached to all nations, that they are witnesses of all the things that pertain to Jesus, that Jesus will send upon them "what my Father promised," but that they are to remain in Jerusalem until they are "clothed with power from on high." Then, one infers, they are to begin the task of witnessing.

Acts repeats all of this information, reminding the reader that Jesus "ordered them not to leave Jerusalem, but to wait there for the promise of the Father," which is now identified as the Holy Spirit (1:4-5). Then Luke recounts Jesus' words in direct speech, "But you will receive power when the Holy Spirit has come upon you; and you will be my witnesses in Jerusalem, in all Judea and Samaria, and to the ends of the earth" (1:8). Several things are highlighted by this repetition: the centrality of Jerusalem in God's promises, the role of the eleven (twelve) as witnesses, and the promise of divine power to those called to this task. These prove to be important themes in the story of the early church. Another theme also emerges rather quickly in the narrative: the near-idyllic unity of the early church.

First the newly commissioned witnesses show their unity of purpose as they return to Jerusalem to await the promised Spirit: "All these were constantly [with one accord: RSV] devoting themselves to prayer, together with certain women, including Mary the mother of Jesus, as well as his brothers" (1:14). After the twelve had been once more fully constituted through the election of Matthias to replace Judas (1:15-26) and they were again "all together in one place" (2:1), the promised Spirit descended on the group. It empowered all to tell "about God's deeds of power" (v. 11) and the twelve especially to proclaim the message of repentance and forgiveness (vv. 14-40). This opening phase of the story of the church then closes with a note concerning the remarkable success of the powerful witnessing of the apostles ("That day about three thousand persons were added," 2:41) and a description of the life-style of the new community of believers:

> They devoted themselves to the apostles' teaching and fellowship, to the breaking of bread and the prayers. Awe came upon everyone, because many wonders and signs were

being done by the apostles. All who believed were together and had all things in common; they would sell their possessions and goods and distribute the proceeds to all, as any had need. Day by day, as they spent much time together in the temple, they broke bread at home and ate their food with glad and generous hearts, praising God and having the goodwill of all the people. And day by day the Lord added to their number those who were being saved. (2:42-47)

This description is structured very carefully. The opening sentence lists four aspects of the believers' life together: devotion to the apostles' teaching, to fellowship, to the breaking of bread, and to prayer. Subsequent verses then elaborate these points in the same sequence. The "awe" that came upon everyone and the "wonders and signs" done by the apostles (v. 43) underscore the power behind the apostolic proclamation. The fellowship *(koinonia)* or spiritual unity of the community is demonstrated by their physical unity as they come together as a community (vv. 44, 46) and especially by the material unity achieved through their practice of holding all things in common *(koina)* (v. 44). The breaking of bread (v. 46) and the prayers (v. 47) of the community are also mentioned again, but in such a way that the description of these activities contributes to the picture of harmonious fellowship. Thus the power of the apostolic witness and the unity of the community of believers both in their devotion to the apostles' word and in their life together are the points emphasized in this initial description. A few chapters later this description of life together is repeated (4:32-37), but with some slight changes in emphasis. To understand the significance of these changes we need to consider briefly the intervening scenes.

CONTESTED POWER AND COMMON GOODS

Four scenes—a miracle, a speech, an arrest, and a reunion—separate the two descriptions of the communal life-style of the church, and these, together with the two scenes that follow them in Acts 5, define the issues that are at stake in this portion of the narrative. Chapter 3 opens with a description of one of the wonders and signs done through the apostles: A man lame from birth is healed by Peter and John. In the speech that follows, Peter makes clear to the astonished crowd what lies behind this miracle: power. The power of Jesus' name, made present through the apostolic witness and released by faith, has made the lame man strong (3:12-16). The speech continues with a call to repentance (vv. 17-26), and while this generates a positive response in many hearers, the religious leaders who are present sense in these men a challenge to their authority. In the next scene (4:1-22) these leaders exercise their own power and have Peter and John arrested. They put a question to the apostles that again makes clear what issue is at stake: "*By what power* or by what name did you do this?" (v. 7, emphasis added).

A conflict is thus developing over the issue of the power shown by the apostles and the authority attendant upon that power. The boldness with which Peter and John respond and the ineffectiveness of the Jewish religious leaders' attempts to restrain them leave no doubt about which side is empowered by God. Moreover, the people respond eagerly to this demonstration of power: Three thousand were baptized the first day (2:41), with more added every day (2:47; 4:4). Indeed, the community of believers (2:47) and especially the apostles (4:21) had such favor with the people that the "rulers of the people" (4:8) seem to be such in name only. Yet the conflict continues, and when Peter and John are reunited with the other apostles, they all pray together with one voice for even more power to meet this opposition (4:23-30). The very room shakes as the prayer is fulfilled (v. 31) and then the narrative is interrupted by a second description of the life-style of the community of believers (vv. 32-37). At first glance these verses seem simply to repeat what had been said earlier, but closer inspection shows that this description is presented in such a way that it contributes to the issues of power and authority that the narrative has just raised.

> Now the whole group of those who believed were of one heart and soul, and no one claimed private ownership of any possessions, but everything they owned was held in common. With great power the apostles gave their testimony to the resurrection of the Lord Jesus, and great grace was upon them all. There was not a needy person among them, for as many as owned lands or houses sold them and brought the proceeds of what was sold. They laid it at the apostles' feet, and it was distributed to each as any had need. There was a Levite, a native of Cyprus, Joseph, to whom the apostles gave the name Barnabas (which means "son of encouragement"). He sold a field that belonged to him, then brought the money, and laid it at the apostles' feet. (4:32-37)

The opening sentence here clarifies what was implicit in the earlier description. Through the disposition of their possessions, the believers indicate their interior disposition. In particular, their unity of heart and soul finds concrete expression in their common sharing of material possessions. Here, though, this unity has new import. Not only does it suggest, as before, the common fellowship of those who share possession of the Holy Spirit, it now signals unity in the face of opposition as well. The lines of conflict have been clearly drawn: The rulers are "gathered together" against the servants of God (4:26), and the community of believers is "of one heart and soul" (4:32) as they face this opposition. This description also makes explicit another point implied in the earlier summary: the power of the apostles' testimony. In the next sentences, however, these two ideas—the unity of the community and the power of the apostles—are brought together to make a new point.

At one level, of course, these verses simply clarify the nature of the community of goods practiced by the Jerusalem community. The members of the community sold what they owned and contributed the proceeds to a common fund, which was administered by the apostles. The process is described in such a way, however, that the act of submitting the proceeds to the community simultaneously reflects submission to the authority of the apostles. This idea is conveyed indirectly but emphatically through the image of the members of the community placing the proceeds from the sale of their possessions "at the apostles' feet" (4:35).

As Johnson has noted, a *person* under or at the feet of another symbolizes in dramatic fashion their respective positions of submission and dominance or authority. The gesture is unambiguous and universal, and both Old and New Testaments are filled with examples of it. Sometimes the gesture signals actual defeat, as when it is promised that enemies will serve as footstools of the Lord's Anointed (Ps. 110:1; Luke 20:43; Acts 2:35). Sometimes it simply suggests an attitude of respect, as in the seating arrangement of a disciple before a teacher (Luke 10:39; Acts 22:3). The basic message of submission to authority, however, remains the same. In our text it is not a person but the person's possessions (or, to be more exact, the money realized from the sale of these possessions) that is placed at the apostles' feet. Yet the basic message of this passage, as we have seen, is that the way one disposes of one's possessions reflects the way one disposes oneself. Thus if sharing possessions in common signaled a common sharing of "heart and soul," placing the proceeds from one's possessions at the apostles' feet symbolized placing one's heart and soul, one's loyalties, there as well. The community is thus described here not simply as united but united under the authority of the apostles, and a contrast is established between opposition to the apostles' authority without and unity and submission to that authority within.

If Luke had mentioned this gesture only once, we might have missed it. But Luke underlines it for his readers by repeating it three times in the space of five verses, first in the general summary (4:35), then in the concrete examples of Barnabas (v. 37) and Ananias (5:2). The story of Ananias provides an especially vivid reminder of the importance of the issues of loyalty and authority that are at stake here.

By any reckoning, the story of Ananias and Sapphira is a strange one. There is nothing else quite like it in the New Testament. It is intended to give a negative example of the early community's sharing of goods and to form a dark counterpoint to the positive model provided by Barnabas. Yet, as we shall see, it actually contradicts in substantial ways the general description it is intended to complement. It also presents a vignette of discipline in the early church that is astonishing for its harshness. "The brief narrative is frankly repulsive," says one commentator, and another adds that it is not only "heartless" but "improbable" as well. Indeed, the story sits somewhat uncomfortably in its context in Acts and in the wider context of the New Testament. But we are not concerned here with questions of historical probability or ethical probity, but with the function of the story in its literary context. Thus we need to look carefully at this story, but we also need to remember that Luke is presenting it in the context of an external challenge to the power and authority of the apostles.

Ananias and Sapphira, we are told, sold a piece of property and then by mutual agreement "brought only a part and laid it at the apostles' feet" (5:2). Peter, as usual the spokesman for the apostles, immediately confronted Ananias with these words:

> Ananias, . . . why has Satan filled your heart to lie to the Holy Spirit and to keep back part of the proceeds of the land? While it remained unsold, did it not remain your own? And after it was sold, were not the proceeds at your disposal? How is it that you have contrived this deed in your heart? You did not lie to us but to God!" (5:3-4)

Upon hearing these words, Ananias fell down and died, and his body was carried out and buried by some members of the community. When Sapphira later implicated herself in the deceit, Peter confronted her too:

> How is it that you have agreed together to put the Spirit of the Lord to the test? Look, the feet of those who have buried your husband are at the door, and they will carry you out. (5:9)

When she heard these words, she too fell down and died and was carried out to be buried beside her husband. The story closes with the comment that "great fear seized the whole church and all who heard of these things" (5:11).

There are a number of striking features to this story. First, Peter's words on the freedom of Ananias and Sapphira to dispose of their property as they saw fit stand in some tension with the earlier statements "*no one* claimed private ownership of any possessions" (4:32) and "*as many* as owned lands or houses sold them" and gave the proceeds to the apostles (4:34). To be sure, nothing in these statements indicates that it was an inviolate *rule* of the community that all members had to contribute their property or proceeds from the property to the community. The text simply observes that all did this. It is still surprising, however, to find the general summaries so quickly contradicted. It is also surprising to discover where the critical moment lies in the process of disposing of one's private property. This moment is not in the decision to sell; that, according to Peter's words, was a free decision. Nor did the critical point lie in the decision over what to do with the proceeds of the sale. That, surprisingly, is also described as a free decision. But once the couple decided on the symbolic gesture of laying the proceeds at the apostles' feet, they could not hold anything back—on pain of death! It was this gesture that marked the point of no return, a gesture that symbolized complete allegiance (heart and soul) to the community and complete submission to the apostles' authority. To symbolize this with only *part* of one's possessions was to make a mockery of the basic notions of community and authority. It was to make a mockery of the Holy Spirit as well, for the power of the Spirit was the source of the apostles' authority. Partial allegiance and partial submission were thus unacceptable, as the fates of Ananias and Sapphira show.

The fate of this couple constitutes a second striking feature of this story. They are both clearly guilty: guilty of bad judgment, greed, and deceit. But serious as these charges are, their punishment seems excessive. They are given no opportunity to repent and they hear no message of forgiveness, yet it was repentance and forgiveness that the apostles were charged to preach. Instead Ananias and Sapphira are struck dead by the powerful word of the apostle. To be sure, attempts have been made to soften the story, to reconcile it with the rest of the New Testament message, to find in it some offer of forgiveness or hint of mercy. An honest reading of the text, however, fails to locate anything like this. Peter proclaims Ananias' guilt and pronounces Sapphira's death sentence ("they will carry you out"). There is no note of pity in the way Luke describes their deaths. There is only the funeral cadence of the young men's feet and Sapphira's body prostrate in death at the feet of the apostle. Irony, not pity, governs this narrative.

Nothing, then, in the way Luke narrates the story of Ananias and Sapphira suggests any criticism of it. It stands as part of his story of the early church, illustrating the authority of its leaders and the necessity for the church to be not just united heart and soul but united heart and soul in their acknowledgment of that authority. Subsequent scenes reinforce the message of the power and authority of the apostles. In the brief summary that follows, for example, Luke emphasizes the miraculous power of the apostles (even Peter's *shadow* is able to heal!), the honor in which they were held, and the multitudes that they added to the church (5:12-16). When the religious authorities try to imprison them once again, they fail utterly and rage in frustration at the apostles' bold retorts (vv. 17-42). Conflict thus develops both within and without the church, but it is completely ineffectual before the awesome power that has been given to the apostles.

CONCLUSIONS

The descriptions in Acts of the Jerusalem church's community of goods and especially the failure of Ananias and Sapphira to embrace wholeheartedly that life-style can thus be read as a part of the story of the power and authority which have been bestowed on the early church and its leaders. At the same time it is hard to escape the conclusion that in this story a theological distortion has occurred. In the first place, the Pauline concept of giving as an expression of fellowship or partnership *(koinonia)* has almost been replaced by giving as a *requirement* of *koinonia*. And the philosophical idea *behind* that, the notion that friends hold all things in common, has almost been subverted by these texts, for the essence of friendship, as Aristotle says, is equality, but the issue *here* is authority. The story of the merciless deaths of two flawed members of the household of faith is also distressing, but the root problem with the story is the cumulative impact of the symbolism and the link that it establishes between power and the disposition of money. At one level Luke's story presupposes the basic insight that "where your treasure is, there your heart will be also" (Luke 12:34). Thus in this narrative the community of goods is a powerful and effective symbol of the unified heart and soul of the early believers. When it is also used as a way of symbolizing the power of the church's leaders, however, the picture becomes distorted. With possessions representing the person and with issues of group loyalty and legitimate authority increasingly dominating the narrative, the disposition of money becomes imbued with theological significance that is far too one-sided. Giving funds becomes a way of acknowledging the power of the church's leaders and the presence of the Holy Spirit in them. Under these circumstances, failure to give funds can only reveal the influence of Satan. The symbolism is too heavy, and while Ananias and Sapphira emerge in the story as vehicles for conveying a message about apostolic power and a warning against greed and fraud, they are also victims of a symbolic world in which power and money are too intimately connected. At the same time, a significant truth is conveyed through this narrative. Issues of power *will* distort requests for funds, and by illustrating this truth Luke suggests an appropriate restraint to the activity of asking for money.

FOR FURTHER READING

This picture of a community of goods in the early church has proved fascinating to generations of scholars, though most have approached it as a historical question rather than a literary and theological one. Robert M. Grant, for example, in his book *Early Christianity and Society* (San Francisco: Harper & Row, Publishers, 1977) asks about the "historical direction" of Luke's accounts of a communal life-style and traces the church's attitude to the practice of sharing possessions through the fifth century. In a fine essay entitled "Community of Goods in the Early Church," found in *The Salvation of the Gentiles: Studies in the Acts of the Apostles* (New York: Paulist Press, 1979), Jacques Dupont explores the background of the concept in Jewish and especially in Greek sources, and Joseph A. Fitzmyer includes in his essay, "Jewish Christianity in Acts in Light of the Qumran Scrolls" in *Studies in Luke-Acts,* ed. L. E. Keck and J. L. Martyn (Nashville: Abingdon Press, 1966), a comparison of the community of goods practiced by the Essenes of Qumran and that depicted in Acts. I have followed here, however, the more literary approach that Luke T. Johnson develops in *The Literary Function of Possessions in Luke-Acts* (Society of Biblical

Literature Dissertation Series 39; Chico, Calif.: Scholars Press, 1977), though his work is far more carefully nuanced than the brief treatment presented here. In a second book, *Sharing Possessions: Mandate and Symbol of Faith* (Philadelphia: Fortress Press, 1981), Johnson reflects more extensively on the theological implications of the ownership and use of possessions. This book, however, covers a wide range of biblical texts, and only a few pages are devoted to the portrait of the early church in Acts.

Schuyler Brown also asks about theological implications in his discussion of the story of Ananias and Sapphira in *Apostasy and Perseverance in the Theology of Luke* (Analecta Biblica 36; Rome: Pontifical Biblical Institute, 1969). His work is helpful in illuminating the continuity of perspective between the gospel and Acts, but he does not explore the way the issue of power has affected the story in Acts. Robert J. Karris, in an essay entitled "Poor and Rich: The Lukan *Sitz im Leben*" in *Perspectives on Luke-Acts,* ed. C. H. Talbert (Danville, Va.: Association of Baptist Professors of Religion, 1978), considers Acts 2:41-47 and 4:31-35 as part of Luke's pervasive concern to address issues of poverty and wealth. Karris, however, tends to treat the passages in isolation from their literary context and thus does not recognize the interplay of themes in the opening chapters of Acts.

The best commentary on Acts remains that of Ernst Haenchen, *The Acts of the Apostles* (Philadelphia: Westminster Press, 1971), though it is somewhat dated. (The English translation rests on a 1965 German edition.) Hans Conzelmann's commentary, recently published in English in the Hermeneia series (Philadelphia: Fortress Press, 1987), is also good, but it too derives from an older German work. Gerhard A. Krodel's commentary in the Augsburg series (Minneapolis, Minn.: Augsburg, 1986) is much more recent, but his goals and bibliography are also much more modest.

For an evaluation of what "authority" means in different

contexts, see E. D. Watt's nice little book *Authority* (New York: St. Martin's Press, 1982). Information on the *Didache* is found at the end of chapter 1. Aristotle's comments on friendship can be found in his *Nicomachean Ethics*, books 8 and 9, which also is mentioned at the end of that chapter.

CONCLUSION

> Now it is superfluous for me to write to
> you about the offering for the saints.
> —II Corinthians 9:1 (RSV)

I t would be superfluous indeed to repeat here the conclusions that have already been drawn at the end of each chapter. And it would be anachronistic to apply these conclusions directly to our situation. The radical itinerancy of the early Palestinian movement, for example, is no longer possible, nor do pastors today have Paul's option of supporting themselves through manual labor instead of accepting remuneration from their churches. Nevertheless, some issues have been raised in our survey of these New Testament texts that merit further reflection in the light of the needs and circumstances of today's churches. Here I simply raise some of the issues. The task of reflection falls to the individual churches.

1. Integrity emerges from these texts as a fundamental issue, not just the moral integrity of fund-raising practices, though that is of utmost importance, but the integrity of these practices within the whole ministry of the church. Like the Cynics, the members of the Palestinian movement and Paul recognized that requests for money should be an extension of the message and ministry of the church. That is, the theological message conveyed by the money-raising practices of a church should be congruent with the gospel proclaimed by that church.

2. In connection with that, the texts also make it clear that requests for money can acquire unanticipated theological

overtones. Indeed, *layers* of theological significance are possible, for the changing circumstances in which requests are made will change the way the requests are heard and the messages they convey. Paul certainly found this to be the case in the rapidly changing circumstances in Corinth, and today's churches should always be alert to the theological implications of their fund-raising efforts. There is, for example, always the possibility of a connection arising between money relations and authority relations, yet this connection is, as we have seen, a potentially destructive one. Even the inevitable link between one's self and one's possessions can, in certain circumstances, convey an inappropriate message.

3. In a different vein, the practices of the early Palestinian mission movement, though so incompatible with the present situation, serve to remind us of the importance of radical trust. We can no longer rely, as they did, on spontaneous hospitality to pay the monthly bills, but if the fund-raising enterprise becomes so elaborate that the fundamental issue of trust is no longer evident, this would seem to be a sign that something is amiss.

4. The concept of reciprocity appeared throughout these texts, often with the aid of elaborate chains or circles of reciprocity, as the fundamental warrant for requests for money. The theological implications of this concept, of course, are widely appreciated today, but they are also often misused. The pattern we see in these New Testament texts is that requests for money were rooted in a prior exchange of spiritual benefits. They were not made with the promise of *generating* these benefits. Furthermore, any benefits that did accrue from the gift, whether material or spiritual, were not to stop with the receiver but were to become the basis for further acts of reciprocity. The implications of Paul's idea of a grace-dynamic operating in requests for money need to be carefully investigated.

5. Likewise, the concept of partnership that emerged in these texts needs to be appropriated with care. Paul, for

example, did not suggest that one becomes a partner in ministry through one's donations but that requests for money are to be rooted in a prior sense of fellowship and partnership that has been established on other grounds altogether. This means that the basic work of fund-raising begins long before any requests are made. The seeds for these requests are planted through every act that creates in the members of the church a sense of mutual trust, shared faith, and common goals. It is then that the act of giving can become a joyous celebration of faith, that the givers benefit more than the receivers, and that the requests for money can be seen by all as a link in the operation of God's grace.

DISCUSSION QUESTIONS

CHAPTER 1

1. In what sense might the Cynic advice to accept gifts only from those who were being benefited be applicable to the church? In what ways does the giver benefit from the act of giving?

2. The Cynics reveled in transgressing society's norms, and their aggressive begging was part of that attitude. Is a countercultural attitude at all appropriate to the church, especially in its fund-raising activities?

3. Benefactors, on the other hand, were a necessary and accepted part of the fabric of ancient society and are important in our own society as well. Is this model of giving and receiving an appropriate one for the church to consider?

4. How does the concept of the reciprocity of gift-giving work in our churches? Is this reciprocity always healthful for all concerned? When might it become unhealthful?

CHAPTER 2

1. Circumstances have changed too much for us to follow literally the life-style prescribed by the mission instructions in the gospels. What message, then, do they convey to us today?

2. What answer do the gospels suggest to the question of how far the church should rely on trust and how far it should

rely on careful financial planning? Are you comfortable with this answer?

3. The *Didache* (pronounced *dih-dah-kay*), with its wary attitude toward traveling missionaries who required support, did not make it into the New Testament canon. Do you think its message *should* have been canonized? Why or why not?

4. Luke's gospel seems to suggest a pattern of gradual accommodation of the mission instructions to changing circumstances. What answer does it suggest to the question of how far the church should go in adopting the ways of the world in pursuing its own stewardship and missions? Do you agree with this suggested limit?

CHAPTER 3

1. In Corinth, Paul took the radical step of refusing payment in order to create no obstacle to the gospel. What might it mean for us today to place no obstacle in the way of the gospel in the church's monetary and fund-raising policies?

2. In II Corinthians, Paul insists that the means of financing the work of the gospel must be an extension of the gospel's message. How might today's churches meet that challenge? Under this criterion, would bake sales and rummage sales be an appropriate means of raising money? Why or why not?

3. Paul perceived a connection between money relations and authority relations. Should generous giving permit a stronger voice in the decision making of the church? On the other hand, shouldn't those who have contributed substantially to a church be expected to show concern about its development, theological and otherwise?

4. When Pat Robertson and Jim and Tammy Faye Bakker called contributors to their ministries "Partners," they were picking up an important aspect of Paul's understanding of

the proper relationship between the givers and receivers of funds in the church. The generous response of people to their requests suggests the power of this concept, but the Bakkers' financial embarrassments also illustrate the dangers inherent in it. What aspects of this concept leave it open to abuse? How might the church properly employ the concept? Does Paul, in your estimation, abuse the concept?

CHAPTER 4

1. The Great Collection acquired several layers of theological meaning which both enhanced and hindered its success. Have you had any fund-raising experiences in which the enterprise took on unexpected theological coloring?

2. It is clear from my presentation that at several points I thought Paul had gone too far in his efforts in Corinth on behalf of the Great Collection. Do you agree? Did the end justify the means?

3. Paul never speaks of tithing as a way of raising money for the church, yet many churches find tithing or some form of proportional giving to be an effective way of meeting the budget. Are there fundamental differences between Paul's understanding of giving in terms of overflowing grace and the concept of percentage giving? Is the perception of grace in today's churches strong enough to serve as a well-spring for giving?

4. Of the various theological concepts that Paul attaches to the act of giving—fellowship, service, ministry, blessing, praise, liturgy—which speaks most effectively to you? Why?

5. A reciprocity or chain of benefaction was fundamental to Paul's understanding of giving, and this reciprocity worked on several levels: between God and humans and between spiritual and material well-being. So often, however, reciprocity is understood in rather simplistic—and self-serving—ways: I will give to the church *so that* God will reward

me. How does *Paul's* understanding of reciprocity differ from this? Is it as effective a concept?

CHAPTER 5

1. If I have read it correctly, the story of Sapphira and Ananias dramatically reveals the dangers that arise when money is too closely linked with authority. Do any of the readings earlier in this book suggest theological resources to help the church resist making this connection in its own financial activities? Are there aspects of your church's worship service that encourage—or discourage—this connection? For example, how are the filled collection plates brought forward and who receives them?

2. What exactly did Ananias and Sapphira do wrong? Was it their greed or deceit or hypocrisy—or something else—that was so blameworthy? Would we evaluate their actions the same way? Should we?

INDEX OF PASSAGES

BIBLE

EARLY CHRISTIAN LITERATURE

OTHER ANCIENT SOURCES